THE NORTH ATLANTIC RIGHT WHALE

Past, Present, and Future

Joann Hamilton-Barry

NIMBUS
PUBLISHING
— NIMBUS.CA —

To Nick Barry, my best friend and the best husband in the world. Together we have done some amazing things and gone to some incredible places. Next on the list is getting up close to some friendly whales. Your encouragement and support has given me the opportunity to pursue my dreams and achieve things that I never thought were possible. Thanks for always being there for me.

~

Nimbus Publishing Limited
3660 Strawberry Hill Street, Halifax, NS, B3K 5A9
(902) 455-4286 nimbus.ca

Printed and bound in Canada

NB1445

Cover photograph: Nick Hawkins Photography
Design: Jenn Embree
Editor: Whitney Moran
Proofreader: Angela Mombourquette

Library and Archives Canada Cataloguing in Publication

Title: The North Atlantic right whale : past, present, and future / Joann Hamilton-Barry.
Names: Hamilton-Barry, Joann, author.
Description: Includes bibliographical references.
Identifiers: Canadiana (print) 20189068523 | Canadiana (ebook) 20189068531 | ISBN 9781771087483 (softcover) | ISBN 9781771087490 (HTML)
Subjects: LCSH: Northern right whale. | LCSH: Northern right whale—Conservation.
Classification: LCC QL737.C423 H36 2019 | DDC 599.5/273—dc23

Nimbus Publishing acknowledges the financial support for its publishing activities from the Government of Canada, the Canada Council for the Arts, and from the Province of Nova Scotia. We are pleased to work in partnership with the Province of Nova Scotia to develop and promote our creative industries for the benefit of all Nova Scotians.

CONTENTS

The North Atlantic right whale is facing extinction; here, a North Atlantic right whale (NARW) puts on a majestic display.
(New England Aquarium)

WHAT IS HAPPENING WITH THE NORTH ATLANTIC RIGHT WHALE?

> "Unless we change things fairly dramatically about how we use the oceans, especially in relation to entanglement, I have a lot of fear about what's going to happen to the right whales."
>
> Amy Knowlton, research scientist, New England Aquarium, *Cape Cod Times*

The North Atlantic right whale is nearly extinct. While estimates vary, there may be as few as 400 left in the world. In 2017, at least 17 of these marine mammals were killed in the waters off the east coasts of Canada and the United States. If this trend continues, they could all be gone before 2040.

Some species of whales have already vanished from our planet. Gray whales disappeared from the Atlantic Ocean in the 1700s and can now only be found in the Pacific Ocean.

Leviathan, ketos, grampus and behemoth are some of the words that have been used when referring to whales.

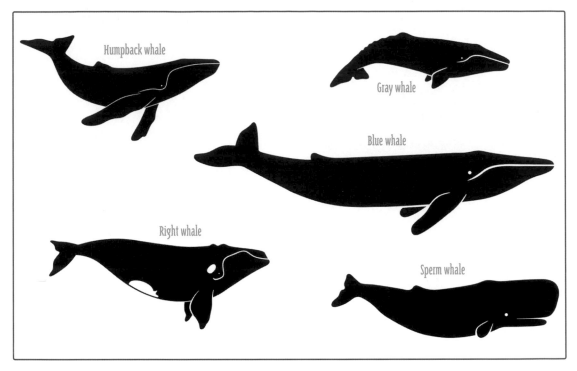

Some species of whales have already vanished. Gray whales can no longer be found in the Atlantic Ocean, for example. This image shows the variation between humpback, gray, blue, right, and sperm whales. **(iStock.com/KBelka)**

The endangered blue whale, at nearly thirty metres long, is the largest animal to have ever existed. While there are 10,000 to 25,000 blue whales remaining in the world, there may be as few as 600–1,000 remaining in Atlantic Canadian waters. Some experts say that there may be fewer than 40 individual North Pacific right whales remaining in the waters off western North America, making it the only large whale more likely to completely disappear than the North Atlantic right whale. Some sources claim that there are only 12 vaquitas, a small porpoise struggling to survive in the Gulf of California, left in the world. In 2006 the baiji, known as the Chinese river dolphin, was declared extinct. After surviving in China's Yangtze River for more than 20 million years, the baiji's disappearance has been directly linked to human impact: overfishing, pollution, boat

The abbreviation NARW will be used when referring to the North Atlantic right whale, one of three species of right whales around the world.

traffic, and habitat destruction. The disappearance of the baiji marks the first extinction of a large mammal species in fifty years. But sadly, it may not be the last.

～

The North Atlantic right whale has been called an "urban whale" because it spends the majority of its time along the eastern coast of Canada and the US, close to some of the busiest ports and active fishing grounds in the world. The proximity of whales and people has been devastating for the NARW, leading scientists Scott Kraus and Rosalind Rolland to coin the term "Urban Whale Syndrome" to describe the whale's plight. The symptoms are: increased mortality from human activities, habitat loss, decreased reproduction, and poor body condition or skin lesions.

Before the summer of 2017, estimates put the population of North Atlantic

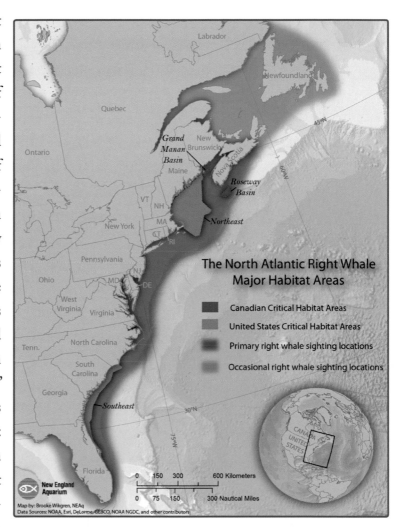

This map depicts many of the major habitat areas of the NARW. Note that it does not emphasize the more recent significance of the Gulf of St. Lawrence; the area shaded in turquoise indicating occasional sightings of right whales may now be one of the two most important habitat areas for right whales. (**New England Aquarium**)

right whales between 425 and 450. With the death of 17 North Atlantic right whales in the summer of 2017, 4 percent of the population disappeared within a few months. To put this into perspective, imagine if everyone in the eight biggest cities in the world disappeared in a single season. With so few of these whales left, scientists fear the species will not be able to survive. Of the remaining whales, fewer than 100 are reproductive females. This is especially concerning to scientists because females have a lower survival rate than males.

With the release of its annual report card in 2018, the North Atlantic Right Whale Consortium (NARWC) determined that there were 411 NARW remaining in the entire population at the end of 2017. Additionally, there were three known deaths in the summer of 2018, and no calves were seen.

One new calf was spotted in the traditional calving grounds off Florida in December 2018. By the end of February 2019, there were a total of 7 new calves. While the birth of 7 new calves is good news indeed, it can't be considered a baby boom. In reality, 2019 is on track to be the fourth worst calving season since 2000, with only a third of the average number of NARW births. On a positive note, by the end of May 2019, a number of adult NARWs and calves were spotted in the Gulf of St. Lawrence.

The right whale has always been a target for whalers. It earned its name as the "right," or correct, whale to kill because it is large, swims slowly at the surface, and often stays close to shore. Early fishers hunted the right whale for its

Baleen

Baleen was often called whalebone but is actually is composed of keratin, the same material that makes up human fingernails. Baleen was first used by Indigenous people to make fishing lines and weirs, snares used in animal trapping, for hunting bows, toboggan runners, and to weave mats and baskets. The Basque whalers are known to have used large baleen plates when constructing the roofs of their buildings in Red Bay, Labrador, in the sixteenth century. Because it could bend and return to its original shape, baleen was a valuable resource used to make corsets, combs, brushes, umbrellas, and fishing rods in the 1700 and 1800s. By the twentieth century, it was replaced by flexible steel, and then plastic. Near the end of the days of commercial hunting of right whales, when baleen was much more valuable than blubber, the head of the whale was saved and the rest of the body discarded.

huge amounts of blubber and valuable baleen, which they called whalebone. And because the right whale floats when dead, whereas other whales sink when killed, it was easy to tow to shore for butchering.

Commercial killing of right whales was banned in 1935. At that time there may have been as few as 100 NARWs left alive. Since then, the population has grown, but not at a steady rate. Only 1 calf was born in 1999–2000. In 2010 there were 481, after a record 39 births the previous season. In 2017–18, no new calves were born. In the past, females would give birth every three to five years; now, the average calving interval is closer to ten years. Scientists fear that females are now only living for thirty years, less than half their potential life span of up to seventy years.

In the past, the most frequent killers of right whales were ships. Large, slow-moving NARWs can't

In the summer of 2018, though no North Atlantic right whales were found dead in Canadian waters, 3 were found in the waters off the eastern US. One was a ten-year-old female, one was a male that was likely one of only five calves born in 2016–17, and the third could only be described as a sub-adult male, as the body was badly decomposed. All three died as a result of entanglement.

In the past, the most frequent killers of right whales were ships. Despite changes to shipping lanes, new rules, and recommendations to reduce ship speed, NARWs continue to be killed as the result of ship strikes. **(iStock.com/shaunl)**

get out of the path of a fast-moving ship. It is unknown how or if right whales detect the potential danger. After much study and cooperation between government and industry, steps have been taken to help protect the right whale. In some cases, as in the Bay of Fundy, shipping lanes have been moved, and an area to be avoided was designated in the Roseway Basin, making it safer for whales. In other areas, mariners are given information about the possible presence of whales and are instructed to reduce speed to avoid collisions.

In areas such as the Gulf of St. Lawrence, there were no protective measures prior to August 2017. In 2018 the mandatory measures were continued, with some modifications, and there were no reports of dead right whales in the Gulf. Despite changing shipping lanes, setting rules, and making voluntary recommendations to reduce ship speeds, NARWs continue to be killed as the result of ship strikes outside protected areas and seasons.

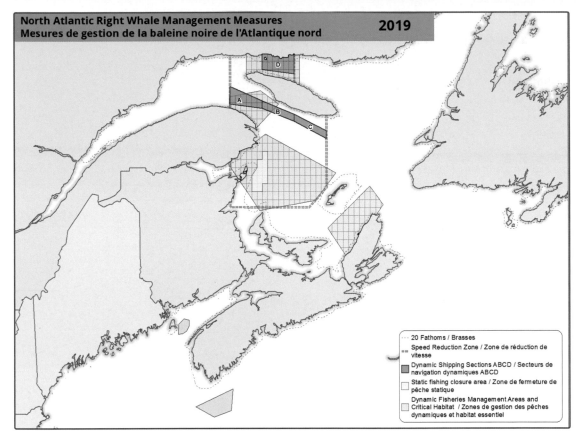

Measures such as fishing closures and speed reduction zones are in place to help protect the North Atlantic right whale. **(Fisheries and Oceans Canada. Reproduced with the permission of © Her Majesty the Queen in Right of Canada, 2019)**

Both NARWs and ships are found in the waters of Atlantic Canada and the eastern US. People can't change the location of the NARW's food, and they can't make the NARWs change their migration paths, but they can change where and how they travel when they are in the home of the NARW.

The leading cause of death of NARWs today is by entanglement in fishing gear. Rope strength has increased since the mid-1990s, and while some whales are able to shed the lines on their own, other whales remain entangled. The stronger rope is cutting into the whales' skin, causing severe injuries that can lead to infection. Dragging lines and gear can make it more difficult for whales to swim, feed, and migrate. Current statistics

This female NARW was born in 2006; she was known as Starboard because she was missing her right fluke blade from an incident involving a ship's prop. Here, she is shown after becoming entangled in fishing gear. **(Image collected under MMPA research permit #21371. Photo Credit: NOAA/NEFSC/Peter Duley)**

show that 83 percent of NARWs have been entangled at least once, and 50 percent more than once. You can read more about recent efforts to address this problem in Chapter 6.

> "As sad as it may sound, there may be a day when the only place that you are going to see a right whale is in a museum."
>
> –Deborah Tobin, author of *Tangled in the Bay: The Story of a Baby Right Whale*

Premature deaths, a decline in fertility, and a dangerous habitat are a catastrophic combination. But there is hope. Governments, scientists, industry members, fishers, conservation groups, and concerned individuals are all working to prevent the extinction of the North Atlantic right whale.

≋ *Delilah* ≋

You can easily spot a North Atlantic right whale in New Brunswick. A life-size fiberglass replica of Delilah, along with her skeleton, is on display in the Hall of the Great Whales at the New Brunswick Museum in Saint John (see page 85).

Delilah was killed by a ship strike in 1992 and towed ashore to Grand Manan, New Brunswick, an island in the Bay of Fundy. Her death provided the impetus for moving the area's shipping lanes. After a careful necropsy by museum and whale scientists and veterinary pathologists, the skeleton was placed in mesh bags and suspended in the ocean to clean the bones. After eight months, the bones were brought to the surface. Further cleaning over a two-year period was required before the skeleton could be reassembled.

Delilah's body on a beach in Grand Manan. In life, Delilah was thirteen metres long and weighed an estimated thirty-seven tonnes. At the time of her death, Delilah was still nursing an eight-month-old calf and they were spending their first summer together in the Bay of Fundy. **(New Brunswick Museum)**

After Delilah was killed in the Bay of Fundy in 1992, her skeleton was placed in mesh bags and suspended in the ocean off Grand Manan to be cleaned. After eight months, the bones were inspected and deemed clean enough to be pulled to the surface. (D.F. McAlpine/New Brunswick Museum)

At the time of her death, Delilah was still nursing an eight-month-old calf and they were spending their first summer together in the Bay of Fundy. When Delilah was killed, the calf disappeared and researchers believed that it had also died. Thrilled to see the calf in the Bay of Fundy the following summer, whale scientist Dr. Moira Brown named it Calvin, after the playful character in the *Calvin and Hobbes* cartoon strip. Calvin the calf was curious and was observed approaching and interacting with boats. Because of Delilah's untimely death, Calvin was forced to stop nursing months earlier than usual for a NARW calf, but somehow managed to survive on other sources of nourishment. In 2005 Calvin returned to the Bay of Fundy with her own calf. She gave birth to a second calf in 2009, and a third in 2015. Like so many other NARWs, Calvin has scars showing that she has suffered at least one entanglement.

In life, Delilah was thirteen metres long and weighed an estimated thirty-seven tonnes. Delilah is #1223 and Calvin is #2223 in the Right Whale Catalog (see pages 30–31).

Delilah's skeleton is the only full North Atlantic right whale on display in Canada and is one of the most popular exhibits at the New Brunswick Museum.

Chapter 1

A BRIEF HISTORY
OF WHALING:
How Did We Get Here?

"The names that we have for whales—sperm whale, right whale, or humpback whale—are quite ugly. They're based on their utility to us, or what we perceive as their physical bizarreness. So even our nomenclature for them is based on a deception, on a denial of their beauty."

–Philip Hoare, author of *The Whale: In Search of the Giants of the Sea* in the *Boston Globe*

People *have been hunting and killing right whales for more than one* thousand years.

For millennia, Indigenous people living near the shores of the world's oceans harvested stranded whales and hunted small whales, taking only what was needed for their survival. This subsistence fishery did not have a lasting negative impact on the whale population.

At the beginning of the last millennium off the coasts of Europe, however, many species of whales, including North Atlantic right whales, were hunted by the Basques in what is now France and Spain. This fishery was not merely for

The Vikings and then the Basque whalers were the earliest Europeans to visit what is now Quebec, Newfoundland, and the Maritime provinces.

Legal subsistence hunting of marine mammals, including some whale species, is still carried out by Indigenous peoples in Canada, the US, and elsewhere. It is considered an integral part of culture and a right of Indigenous people. Indigenous hunts are regulated under government quotas and the meat is not sold commercially.

subsistence. The whales were sold for food and their oil as fuel for lamps. The early Basque commercial whaling industry featured watchtowers with a commanding ocean view, so that small boats could be quickly launched when a whale was sighted. By the nineteenth and into the early twentieth century, whale oil was used for making soap, candles, cosmetics, and even margarine. The bones and remains of many species of whales were used in fertilizer, pet food, and even human food. During the Second World War, at restaurants in London, England, it was possible to buy a "Waleburger steak." In his book *The Whale: In Search of the Giants of the Sea*, author Philip Hoare suggests that "waleburger" may have been spelled incorrectly to obscure the fact that the meat was from a whale.

Pre-exploitation population estimates of the number of right whales range from novelist Farley Mowat's high of 200,000 to 12,000–15,000 by right whale expert Dr. David Gaskin. Scientists now feel that the actual number may be even lower and that there could have been fewer than 2,000 right whales before commercial whaling began.

At first, in the eleventh century, the Basques ventured up and down the coast of Europe in open dories. But what began as a shore-based fishery eventually expanded into a pelagic, or offshore, fishery. Fishers from other European nations also began to hunt whales. As the number of whales diminished in their waters, the Basques set their course farther afield. By the sixteenth century, they had crossed the North Atlantic to establish seasonal fishing stations in Newfoundland and Labrador.

Throughout the sixteenth and seventeenth centuries, Basque whalers targeted bowhead whales, and possibly also caught right whales, from summer into fall in the Strait of

Greenland or Right Whale (*Balœna mysticetus*).

This engraving depicts a Southern right whale being hunted during the early days of commercial whaling. (iStock.com/*duncan1890*)

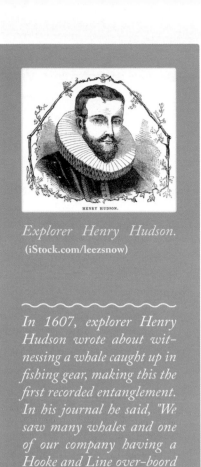

In 1607, explorer Henry Hudson wrote about witnessing a whale caught up in fishing gear, making this the first recorded entanglement. In his journal he said, "We saw many whales and one of our company having a Hooke and Line over-boord to trie for Fish, a Whale came under the Keel of our ship and made her held, yet by Gods mercie we had no harme, but the losse of the hooke and three parts of the line."

Belle Isle, between the coasts of what is now Newfoundland and Labrador. The Basques are credited with being the first to process whale blubber into oil onboard their large ships. With this system they could stay at sea longer, catch more whales, and process more oil. Furthermore, knowing the mother whale's reluctance to leave her baby would ensure an easy kill, the Basques employed a technique that saw the right whale calf killed first. While this method was efficient, it led directly to the decimation of the right whale population. Some historians estimate that between 1530 and 1610, approximately 400 whales were caught each year. This seasonal hunt was clearly unsustainable. By the early seventeenth century, it became more difficult to catch whales in this area. Basque whaling in the New World drew to a close as ships began to return to Europe only half full.

As mentioned earlier, historians believe Indigenous peoples living along the coast of North America participated in subsistence whaling before the *Mayflower*, carrying English Puritans (Pilgrims), landed at Cape Cod in 1620. While the Pilgrims could see whales in the water close to their shores, they didn't begin the difficult task of trying to catch large whales until the middle of the seventeenth century.

Coastal whaling began off what is now Long Island, New York. As the industry grew, open dories were exchanged for larger ships that could remain at sea for seven to ten days. Similarly, whaling in Massachusetts Bay, Cape Cod, and Nantucket began with

Nantucket Sleigh Ride

During the early days of commercial whaling, whalers typically hunted with harpoons: barbed, spear-like missiles with rope attached. With a harpoon embedded in its body, an injured whale would flee, trying to escape its hunters. At any time during the hunt, the whale could crush the small, open boat and kill everyone with a flick of its huge tail. Early whalers knew that if the harpoon stayed in place and they could hold on, the whale would eventually tire and stop swimming. As a result, whalers could be pulled behind the whale for hours—a long and dangerous feat known as the "Nantucket sleighride."

Once the whale finally stopped, the harpooner repeatedly stabbed it behind the flipper. With the heart and lungs pierced, the whale would spout blood from its blow hole. The excited crew knew this meant the animal was dying and someone would shout, "There's fire in the chimney!" The crew would row back to their ship, towing the dead whale, where they would begin the long process of harvesting the blubber to make oil for lamps.

Scrimshaw

Beginning in the 1800s, as a way to pass time on long voyages, whalers began decorating the teeth and bones of whales with inscriptions and carving. Known as scrimshaw, the items became popular collectibles. Former US president John Kennedy kept his favourite pieces of scrimshaw on his desk in the Oval Office. After he was assassinated in 1963, he was buried with a piece of scrimshaw featuring the presidential seal.

a shore fishery. As the number of whales found inshore declined, by the mid-eighteenth century, whalers ventured farther offshore, as far south as the Bahamas and Florida. With the outbreak of the American Revolution in 1765, whaling ceased, mainly due to British blockades of some harbours. Many men left to fight and others used their whale boats to attack British encampments.

From the end of the 1700s until the mid-1860s, American whalers were sailing as far as the Pacific Ocean and the shores of the African continent in search of whales. These voyages could last three to four years. The American Civil War (1861–1865) again put a temporary halt to whaling, but it was the discovery of petroleum in 1859 that signalled the eventual demise of the use of whale oil. Petroleum is the flammable oil found in some sedimentary rocks that, when processed, makes a clean burning fuel. This new product did not have the pungent odour created when burning blubber from right whales, and quickly became cheaper than whale oil.

~

"Without exception, no species of great whale was persecuted for so long and so intensely as the right whale, and this unhappy legacy has left us with an animal that is on the brink of extinction in two of the three oceans which it inhabits."

–Phil Clapham, *Right Whales: Natural History & Conservation*

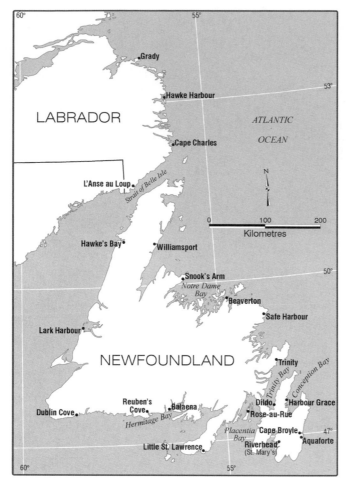

Newfoundland and Labrador whaling stations, 1898-1972.
(Dickinson and Sanger)

Early commercial whaling in what is now Canada was centred in the Strait of Belle Isle, as described earlier, with the Basques. In the 1700s, American and European fishers caught whales off the coast of Atlantic Canada, and in the 1800s a whaling station was established in Newfoundland. By the early 1900s more than a dozen whaling stations were located on the island, where the whales caught off its coasts were processed. The only commercial station outside of Newfoundland was located in Blandford, Nova Scotia, near Halifax. Karl Karlsen and Company was established in the late 1940s to process seal, and from the 1960s to the 1970s it also processed whales.

The Bay of Fundy has been a perfect environment for copepods (see page 29) and the whales who feast on them, but whaling was not an important commercial fishery there, even given the proximity to New England. While the historic record indicates that New England whalers occasionally caught right whales here in the 1700s, it was not a typical hunting ground for them. The high tides and dense fog may have kept the nearby New England whalers from the area, creating a refuge for the whales. This combination of fog and tides may have saved the NARW from extinction.

Flensing a whale in Williamsport, Newfoundland, September 30, 1949. (Gert Crosbie Photograph Collection, Maritime History Archive, Memorial University of Newfoundland)

In 1909, the last right whale was killed by whalers off Cape Cod after it became entangled in fishing gear. It was taken to Boston and put on display, as it was a rare catch, even then, since the number of right whales caught each year had been steadily diminishing. The last right whale hunted in southern American waters was killed off the coast of Florida in 1935 (see Whale #1045 sidebar below). By the time the commercial killing of the right whale was banned that same year, there may have been as few as—or fewer than—50 to 100 North Atlantic right whales left in the world.

≡ *Whale #1045* ≡

Whale #1045 was considered to be "irregular," as it was only seen by scientists six times between 1959 and 1995.

A newspaper article published in the *New York Herald Tribune* on March 31, 1935, featured a sad story of a right whale mother and calf. When fishers looking for tuna came across two whales, they shot at them with a rifle for more than six hours, but the mother wouldn't leave her calf. After being repeatedly harpooned, the calf finally died. In spite of all of her own wounds, the mother right whale didn't leave until her calf's body was tied next to the boat. This calf was the last reported NARW to be hunted and killed. Reports at the time stated that the captain just wanted to be able to say that he had caught a whale.

The newspaper article featured a photo of the mother with clearly visible and unique markings. In 1959, two scientists from the Woods Hole Oceanographic Institution conducting a right whale study in Massachusetts Bay photographed a lone right whale. Another scientist, with the New England Aquarium, was amazed to find that they had a match. It was whale #1045 from the newspaper photo!

Whale #1045 was last spotted alive in 1995 off Georges Bank, south of Nova Scotia, with a propeller wound on her head. Since she had a calf in the original photo, it was estimated that she was ten years old at the time, and therefore would have been born in 1925. This demonstrates that whale #1045 lived at least seventy years.

The last time a right whale was hunted and killed in Canadian waters was in May 1951, off Trinity Bay, Newfoundland.

Despite the nearly century-long ban on killing right whales, individual whales continue to die as a result of interaction with humans. Read on to learn more about the biology of the NARW and why it was such an attractive target for whalers, and check out the timeline starting on page 90 for more information on the history of whaling and conservation efforts.

Chapter 2

BIOLOGY: What Do We Know About the North Atlantic Right Whale?

"With its baroque, glossy body encrusted with callosities, its paddle-shaped flippers and its bizarre, yawning mouth filled with baleen, *Eubalaena glacialis* is both grotesque and wondrous."

–Philip Hoare, *The Whale: In Search of the Giants of the Sea*

Perhaps one of the most surprising things about whales is that they evolved from land animals. Beginning 50 to 60 million years ago, condylarths lived near and began spending more time in the water, possibly to escape predators. Over millions of years, these small land animals evolved into marine animals with the development of flippers in place of front legs. Their bodies lengthened and became more streamlined. The only evidence of whales' former back legs are the vestigial pelvic bones. During these millions of years, the nose (blow hole) moved to the top of the head to make breathing at the water's surface easier and more efficient. Over time, these creatures stay underwater for longer and longer periods.

Aristotle, the ancient Greek scientist and philosopher, born in 384 BCE, may have been the first whale-watcher to record and publish his observations on the biology of dolphins.

The condylarths are the ancestors of all cetaceans (whales) and ungulates (including horses, cattle, pigs, deer, giraffes, rhinoceroses, and hippopotami).

Today, whales are classified in the order *Cetacea*, which includes dolphins, porpoises, and whales of all sizes. Cetaceans are divided into two suborders: *Odontocetes* and *Mysticetes*, which developed about 35 million years ago. *Odontocetes* includes the more than eight species of toothed whales, such as dolphins, porpoises, sperm whales, pilot whales, and orca whales. These whales use high-frequency sound to echolocate, and use their teeth to catch and eat fish, squid, and even seals. *Mysticetes* encompasses the approximately fifteen species of baleen whales, who feed by swimming through the water with their mouths open. Baleen whales take in food by gulping single mouthfuls of water containing prey, sucking bottom organisms from the ocean floor, or filter-feeding continuously while swimming through shoals of plankton such as copepods or krill. Once the food is in their mouths, they use their tongues to push the water out, against the baleen plates, trapping various species of fish, krill, and tiny copepods in their mouths.

Rorqual is the largest suborder of baleen whales, which includes the minke, fin, sei, and humpback. It also includes the blue whale, the largest animal that has ever lived. These whales have distinct grooves on the throat that expand to hold water when they feed.

Types of Right Whales

Fossil records show that the first animals to look like modern whales appeared around 20 million years ago. The skeleton of the modern whale shows how similar the bones in its flippers are to those of other mammals with hands, including humans (see photo on page 25).

Today, there are three distinct species of right whales: North Pacific right whale (*Eubalaena japonica*), Southern right whale (*Eubalaena australis*), and North Atlantic right whale (*Eubalaena glacialis*). Originally, all right and bowhead whales were grouped together as a single species. In 2000, DNA samples indicated that Northern and Southern right whales are actually separate species. It has also been proven that the two types of Northern right whales are different species. Indeed, the North Pacific right whale is more similar to the Southern right whale than it is to the North Atlantic right whale. There are two populations of North Pacific right whales: the Bering Sea population, which may have fewer than 30 whales, and the Sea of Okhotsk population, which may have 100–200 whales. These two Northern right whales are the most endangered of all large whales and are among the most endangered animal species in the world.

"Cetacean" is from the Greek word ketos, meaning "sea monster."

The bowhead whale (*Balaena mysticetus*) closely resembles the right whale but is considered a separate species. The pygmy right whale (*Caperea marginata*) is not related to right whales at all and is the smallest of the baleen whales. Palaeontologists have referred to it as "a living fossil," as it is most closely related to an extinct whale family, the *Cetotheriidae*.

The bowhead whale closely resembles the right whale but is considered a separate species. (iStock.com /ilbusca)

> "To the uninitiated, the right whale can be odd and confusing in appearance. It is a large, relatively rotund whale, with a square chin and a large head that accounts for 25 percent of the total body length in adults. A strongly arched jaw and narrow rostrum (upper jaw) and a bowed lower jaw are characteristic of the species, giving the impression that the whale is 'upside down'."
>
> –Scott D. Kraus and Rosalind M. Rolland, "Right Whales in the Urban Ocean," *The Urban Whale*

The North Atlantic right whale is one of the largest of the great whales. Whales are mammals, and like all other mammals they breathe air and their young are born live. Mother NARWs nurse their calves for about ten to twelve months. The pair forms a strong bond, and mothers have been observed stroking and cradling their calves. Playful calves have been seen butting heads and trying to swim up on their mother's

North Atlantic Right Whale

Classification: Mammals

Order: *Cetacea* (Whales, dolphins, and porpoises)

Suborder: *Mysticeti* (Baleen whale)

Family: *Balaenidae* (Right whale)

Genus: *Eubalaena*

Species: *Glacialis*

Scientific Name: *Eubalaena glacialis*, translation: "true whale of the ice"

Common name: North Atlantic right whale

Size: average of 17 metres in length, and weighing 60-70,000 kilograms; females are slightly larger than males

Age span: unknown, up to 70 years

Diet: Copepods

Habitat: Atlantic Ocean. While some NARWs have been seen off Iceland and Norway and in the Gulf of Mexico, over the last fifty years the typical range is thought to be between the Gulf of St. Lawrence, the Bay of Fundy, and the coast of North America as far south as northern Florida

Threats: Humans

Status: Endangered

Each adult NARW has a distinct pattern of callosities—irregularly shaped, raised and roughed patches of cornified growths—on its head. (Laurie Murison)

back. (See page 38 for more about the early life of the NARW.)

The NARW is described by some as stocky, with its head making up a quarter of its black body. About a third of NARWs have white patches on the belly and throat. Its flippers have been described as paddle-like and it has no dorsal fin. The tail stock is narrow, with a wide and smooth fluke (tail) that can measure six metres across, from tip to tip.

Each adult has a distinct pattern of callosities—irregularly shaped, raised and roughed patches of cornified growths—on the head. Callosities develop in the calf's first few months of life, by eight to ten months old, and are typically the means by which individual whales are distinguished. Three species of whale lice, or cyamids, live on the callosities and feed on the whale's dead skin. The different

> *The NARW is no longer a true "whale of the ice" as it has been hunted to the point that it is no longer found in the cold Arctic waters.*

About a third of NARWs have white patches on the belly and throat. **(Laurie Murison)**

The NARW's flippers are sometimes described as paddle-like. **(Laurie Murison)**

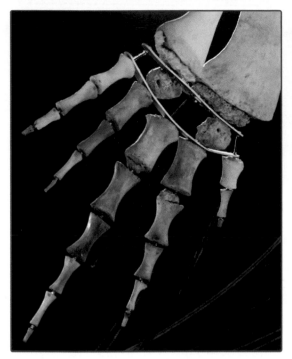

The bones in a whale flipper show many similarities to a human hand. These are Delilah's bones, on display at the New Brunswick Museum in Saint John. (Barry Henderson)

The eye of an adult NARW is about the size of a grapefruit.

species of cyamids vary in colour (white, yellow, or orange) and their presence gives the callosities their colour. Cyamids can be transferred from whale to whale during courtship activities or when a mother is caring for her calf. (For more on callosities in whale identification, see page 30.)

The NARW is a baleen whale. Hanging from each side of the upper jaw is a row of closely spaced, hard but flexible plates of approximately two metres in length. Approximately two hundred and sixty individual plates of baleen make up the full complement in a right whale's mouth. The inside edge of each plate supports a fringe (the braided edge) about twenty-five centimetres long. Baleen can vary in colour from light brown to auburn.

Two blow holes produce the NARW's distinct, bushy V-shaped blow, which can reach up to seven metres when the whale surfaces. While a blow makes the whale appear to be spouting water, like a fountain, it is actually compressed hot, moist air from the whale's lungs that condenses when it meets the cooler air and is no longer under pressure. After surfacing to breathe, the NARW can stay under water for ten to twenty minutes. Because the NARW sleeps at the surface, it can be sometimes mistaken for floating debris. Since a sleeping whale resembles a floating log, this behaviour is called "logging."

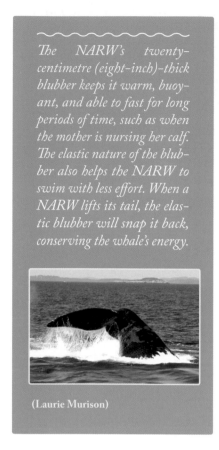

The NARW's twenty-centimetre (eight-inch)-thick blubber keeps it warm, buoyant, and able to fast for long periods of time, such as when the mother is nursing her calf. The elastic nature of the blubber also helps the NARW to swim with less effort. When a NARW lifts its tail, the elastic blubber will snap it back, conserving the whale's energy.

(Laurie Murison)

Hanging from each side of the NARW's upper jaw is a row of approximately two hundred and sixty hard but flexible plates of baleen.
(Laurie Murison)

Diet and Migration

The NARW feeds on tiny crustaceans called copepods. Once it finds a dense aggregation of food, the whale feeds by opening its mouth as it swims forward. Some have described the NARW as looking a lot like a vacuum as it pushes along, taking in huge quantities of copepod-rich water. The tongue forces the water out of the mouth between the baleen plates. The baleen fringe acts as a sieve, retaining the copepods in the mouth and filtering out almost everything else. Adult NARWs may consume to 2,500 kilograms of copepods (about 1 billion) a day.

For the past forty years, scientists have been tracking NARW migration. Yet they are not certain how these whales manage to find their food. Do they follow the patterns of the ocean currents and the topography of the sea floor to learn where to find copepods?

Two blow holes produce the NARW's distinct, bushy V-shaped blow. **(Laurie Murison)**

While a blow makes the whale appear to be spouting water, it is actually compressed hot, moist air from the whale's lungs that condenses when it meets the cooler air and is no longer under pressure. **(Laurie Murison)**

Once it finds a dense aggregation of food, the NARW feeds by opening its mouth as it swims forward. **(Moira Brown)**

No matter what the answer is, as ocean water and the earth's temperature are changing, so too are the locations where copepods are likely to flourish.

All summer and into the early fall, large numbers of NARWs feed in the cool waters of the Gulf of St. Lawrence, the Bay of Fundy, the Roseway Basin (off Yarmouth, Nova Scotia), the Gulf of Maine to Cape Cod Bay, and elsewhere where copepods are plentiful. If a calf spends its summer in these areas, it will likely later return there as an adult. In the late fall, pregnant female and juvenile right whales move to the waters off Florida and Georgia. While in these calving grounds, NARWs fast and live off their fat reserves until the next spring. The larger size of the female may help her to store the extra energy she needs to nurse her calf, whom she'll remain with for twelve to seventeen months. In the late winter, these NARWs begin migrating from the waters of the southeast US, up the coast to spend the spring in Cape Cod Bay and the Gulf of Maine and the summer in the Bay of Fundy, the Gulf of St. Lawrence, and off the coasts of Nova Scotia and northern New England. While this is an established pattern for mothers and calves, it is not the case for most right whales. The winter location of most right whales—the non-calving adult females, juveniles, and males—is unknown. In the mid- to late winter and spring, many of these NARWs appear in Cape Cod Bay.

> When two or three whales feed together, they swim forward in a staggered line called an "echelon formation."

What Are Copepods?

Copepods are plankton, specifically zooplankton (animal plankton), which includes algae, protozoa, tiny invertebrates, and even jellyfish that drift in the ocean. Phytoplankton, or plant plankton, on the other hand, is the plankton that lives near the surface and converts sunlight into energy. Though usually found at or near the water's surface, copepods go through a period of hibernation called a "diapause" in the spring and summer and sink to the ocean floor. When in the Bay of Fundy, NARWs must dive to the ocean floor to find concentrations of copepods. Scientists have recorded seeing whales surface with mud on their heads, indicating that they dove one to two hundred metres down to reach the ocean bottom. These dives can last up to twenty minutes.

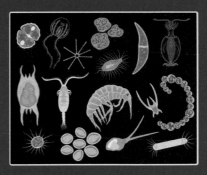

The NARW feeds on tiny crustaceans called copepods. **(iStock.com/ luplupme)**

Many species of copepods are the size of a grain of rice, but some can reach up to one centimetre in length. Climate warming and changing ocean conditions may reduce copepod density in some areas, which is another major concern for the future of the NARW, as they are the whale's main food source.

About a third of NARWs don't follow typical migration paths and scientists don't know where, in the vast Atlantic Ocean, they spend their year. NARW migration patterns may be changing from those which scientists have observed over the last forty years. Climate change may be affecting the supply and location of copepods' food supplies, meaning that whales are moving to where their food is more plentiful. Scientists worry that this will cause them to expend more energy and to be less healthy and able to reproduce.

Each right whale develops callosities on the head, in roughly the same places where humans have hair: on the top of the head, above the eyes, around the mouth, and on the chin. A callosity is hardened skin (think of the back of your heel or the callouses on the side of your big toe) known as "cornified epithelium" that on a right whale is produced as jagged, crusty patches.

The callosities are black but appear to vary in colour based on the species, density and colour of cyamids, or whale lice, present. The unique shapes and patterns of callosities help scientists identify individual whales in the same way fingerprints are used to identify humans. Some whales have even been named after the patterns of their callosities. The NARW "Star" has a star-shaped mark on her head, and "Rat" has a callosity that resembles a rat chasing a ball.

No one is sure exactly why right whales have callosities, but these different callosity patterns, and other data, have been recorded and compiled into a catalogue—or a who's who—of NARWs.

Each right whale develops callosities on the head, in roughly the same places where humans have hair. The presence of different species of cyamids gives the callosities their colour. **(Laurie Murison)**

The unique shapes and patterns of callosities help scientists identify individual whales in the same way fingerprints are used to identify humans. **(Laurie Murison)**

Right Whale Catalog

One of the most important projects of the New England Aquarium (NEAq), located in Boston, Massachusetts, is the compilation and upkeep of the Right Whale Catalog. Beginning in the 1980s,

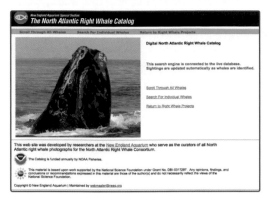

Researchers from the New England Aquarium in Boston have been collecting data about individual right whales for the Right Whale Catalog since the 1980s. (New England Aquarium)

researchers from the NEAq started collecting data about individual right whales, noting callosity patterns, scars, and other distinct markings. Each whale is assigned a number based on when it is first seen. Names are assigned to some whales, usually based on unique anatomical features, including distinctive scarring or healed injuries. The catalogue includes about 1 million images and details of right whale sightings. Some of the whales in the catalogue have been seen every year during the annual Bay of Fundy survey. Others, spotted only twice, years apart, have left scientists to wonder where they go and why their migration patterns differ from those of most other right whales.

Learning More Through Necropsy

A necropsy is a dissection of a dead animal, typically performed in order to learn the cause of death. In the case of the NARW, the goal is to use this information to prevent similar tragedies in the future. A necropsy can sometimes reveal injuries such as broken bones, bruising, and internal hemorrhaging, indicating the right whale may have been struck by a ship.

A necropsy of an animal the size of a NARW is challenging, and can involve a team of up to a dozen people, including veterinarians, biologists, grad students, curatorial and zoology assistants, staff from a variety of government agencies, and even heavy machinery operators. Given the animal's immense size, the necropsy is usually performed close to where the body has washed

Right whales can be identified from airplanes because the unique callosities found on the tops of their heads are visible from the air.

Researchers gather data on a group of North Atlantic right whales. The New England Aquarium's North Atlantic right whale research program is the oldest of its kind. (New England Aquarium)

A researcher observing a whale from the bow of a research vessel. (New England Aquarium)

ashore. When a dead whale is found in a remote or rocky location, it may be necessary to tow the body to a more convenient location. Once the body, which may weigh more than thirty-five tonnes, is accessible, excavators and bulldozers are used to move it above the high-tide mark to give investigators easy access.

Standard necropsy protocol begins with photos and measurements. Samples are taken for testing and, when possible, an identification made; ultimately, the Right Whale Catalog will be updated accordingly. If the whale is entangled, the team photographs the gear and rope while it is wrapped around the whale's body. The gear is carefully removed, measured, and photographed again. Extensive notes are made about the length, thickness, and types of rope found. Records of the specific buoys and traps still attached to the whale are also noted. If enough of the gear remains, an effort is

A necropsy of an animal the size of a NARW is challenging, and requires a strong stomach; here, a team from the New Brunswick Museum measures the body of Delilah, who was killed by a ship strike in 1992 and towed ashore to Grand Manan. (**Laurie Murison New Brunswick Museum**)

Grand Manan fisherman Ken Ingersoll oversees Delilah being loaded for transport to a necropsy site on Grand Manan **(D.F. McAlpine/New Brunswick Museum)**

made to determine where it originated. The marks on the gear may indicate who owns it, allowing scientists to determine where the gear was last used. In Canada, the Department of Fisheries and Oceans (DFO) attempts to track the owners of gear to determine if the gear had been lost or where it may have been set. Knowing these facts may help to determine how and where the whale became entangled. This investigation may lead to changes in the location of fishing zones and spur the development of changes to gear that will ultimately help protect right whales.

A necropsy on an animal this size can take days and can be severely impacted by the weather. The heat of the summer can accelerate decomposition. Freezing temperatures can make it nearly impossible to remove flesh so bones can be examined for fractures. If you have ever smelled a dead fish, try to imagine a rotting carcass weighing thousands of kilograms, sitting for days in the hot summer sun. Dr. Donald McAlpine, head of zoology at the New Brunswick Museum, and a member of the team who worked on the necropsy of Delilah, says "a strong stomach and a weak nose" are helpful if you are working on a necropsy. The work is physically demanding: one must wield large, razor-sharp knives for hours at a time and move heavy pieces of blubber. A dead whale can be smelled for kilometres and deter people

The ocean is vast and it is estimated that only one-third of the whales that die are ever found. As when other sea creatures die and their bodies end up on the ocean floor, a NARW carcass will provide nourishment and even shelter for other marine species. This newly created ecosystem is know as a whale fall.

Studying NARWs in Atlantic Canada

Veterinary pathologists from the Atlantic Veterinary College (AVC), University of Prince Edward Island, directed the necropsies of some of the NARWs that died in waters off Atlantic Canada in the summer of 2017. There are five vet schools in Canada and the AVC is the only one east of Montreal.

The Canadian Wildlife Health Cooperative (CWHC) Atlantic, housed at the AVC, advises and assists various levels of government on issues related to the health of wildlife, especially marine animals and endangered species. In the summer of 2017 the CWHC, AVC, Marine Animal Response Society (MARS), Department of Fisheries and Oceans (DFO), Dalhousie University, Canadian Whale Institute, New Brunswick Museum, and others collaborated to investigate the mass mortality of NARWs off the east coast of North America.

from using the beach or waterfront properties, so there is usually pressure to complete the necropsy as quickly as possible.

Once the necropsy has been completed, decisions have to be made about safely disposing of tonnes of rotting flesh. When possible, individual bones or entire skeletons are retained for preservation in muscums, for further study, or for educational exhibits. Other tissues, parasites, organs, and stomach contents may also be preserved for future study. These collections are immensely important because, as you'll see in the next chapter, there is still so much we don't know about the elusive North Atlantic right whale.

Death by Entanglement

Crab traps like these can weigh more than 360 kilograms; one NARW was seen with four crab traps attached to the ropes that had entangled her.
(Ken Boehner)

Two of the right whales necropsied in the summer of 2017 had been entangled in a considerable amount of rope and gear. One whale, #4504, a two year-old female, was caught in more than 152 metres of rope and was pulling a snow crab trap that was approximately 1.8–2.4 metres (6–8 feet) in diameter. This whale drowned as a result of the entanglement. Another whale, #3603, known as Starboard, was entangled in more than 30 metres of rope and two buoys. Before her death, she was seen with four crab traps (each of which can weigh more than 360 kilograms, or 800 pounds) attached to the ropes that had entangled her.

≋ *Slash* ≋

Slash was first seen in Massachusetts Bay in 1979 and earned her name as she was missing a part of her fluke, likely the result of an encounter with ship's propeller. Slash seems to have learned that ships equal danger, and is known to flee at the sight of any sort of boat. Scientists have wondered if Slash passed this fear on to her several calves. It is believed that whales transmit knowledge, such as the locations of good feeding grounds, to their offspring. It seems possible, therefore, that a fear of ships could also be passed on.

Slash died in 2011. Her body was seen off the coast of Virginia and it is thought that she died from a ship strike. Slash is #1303 in the Right Whale Catalog.

Chapter 3

BEHAVIOUR:
Why Don't We Know
More About Whales?

"It is both frustrating and fascinating that after two decades of intensive study of this small population, researchers still do not know the answers to some basic questions about the life history of the North Atlantic right whale."

–Lance P. Garrison, *The Urban Whale, "The Big Picture: Modeling Right Whales in Space and Time"*

North Atlantic right whales have probably been spending their summers in the Bay of Fundy for thousands of years. But spotting a free-swimming NARW is a bit like finding a needle in a haystack. Even in a body of water as contained as the Bay of Fundy, it is not easy to see a mammal that spends 95 percent of its time underwater.

Thanks to the work of University of New Brunswick scientists Bruce S. Wright and David J. Neave, right whales were confirmed to be in the Bay of Fundy in 1966. Wright and Neave were studying harbour porpoises and had asked ferry boat operators to record sightings of porpoises and any other cetaceans. A report of fifteen right whale sightings in the mouth of the Bay of Fundy came from the ferry boat MV *Bluenose*, travelling between Yarmouth, Nova Scotia, and Bar Harbor, Maine. Wright and Neave mentioned this sighting in their harbour-porpoise research, but other scientists did not consider the sightings to be credible, claiming that reports from mariners with no formal training or experience in identifying whales at sea could not be taken as confirmation. Wright and Neave countered by saying that they had trained the observers and provided them with field guides to aid in identifying different whale species.

Just a few years later, in 1972, scientists from the University of Guelph studying harbour porpoises in the Bay of Fundy near Saint Andrews, New Brunswick, reported that there could be as many as 30 right whales in that part of the Bay.

Soon after, when there were preliminary plans to construct an oil refinery in Eastport, Maine, a short distance from Campobello Island, off New Brunswick, detailed surveys of marine mammals were conducted along the eastern coast of North America and into the Bay of Fundy. In 1979, the Cetacean and Turtle Assessment Program conducted aerial surveys, indicating that there were NARWs summering in the Bay of Fundy. In 1980 the New England Aquarium (NEAq) began its annual surveys and cataloguing of the whales in this area. Once scientists found out where the NARW went in the summer, they began to study their migration patterns, biology, and behaviour.

Mating, Calving, and Early Life

NARWs differ from other great whales as they engage in what appear to be mating activities throughout the year. These are called surface-active groups (SAGs). Females make a specific sound, which scientists describe as being similar to a cow mooing, that can be heard by males at distances of up to ten kilometres or more. Males rush in to approach the female and will even push each out of the way as they compete for the spot nearest the female. The female lies on her back to avoid the males, but must flip over to breathe every minute or so. When she does, individual males jostle for an opportunity to mate. Since most NARW calves are born from December to mid-February, and NARWs are pregnant for twelve to thirteen months, most SAGs do not lead to

Whales and Dolphins, Playing Together

Right whales and dolphins have been spotted playing together in the Bay of Fundy. Scientist Laurie Murison has described what looked like a giant aquatic carousel with whales and dolphins, instead of horses. In the 1990s, she saw a group of more than twenty dolphins and six NARWs swimming in a large circular pattern. The dolphins would appear and disappear, followed by the right whales, which would surface, roll on their sides, and then dive. This activity went on for about fifteen minutes before it broke down into a SAG that included only the right whales.

pregnancy. Conception, therefore, must be taking place in the late autumn to early winter, in an unknown location.

A SAG can be as brief as a few minutes or as long as several hours. It can involve up to 40 males, including those too young to reproduce, and one or two females. Dr. Susan E. Parks and other scientists have found that male NARWs make a sound that that is

Researchers have suggested that females use SAGs as a way of selecting mates who are agile, strong, and good at holding their breath. **(Laurie Murison)**

Male NARWs have the largest testes (up to 500 kilograms each) and among the longest penises (up to three metres) in the entire animal world. Large genital size is the result of evolutionary selection via a process known as "sperm competition," meaning that the individual whale who can produce the largest number of spermatozoa has the best chance of fertilizing a female.

similar to a loud gunshot when in the midst of a SAG. These gunshot sounds may be made to attract females, signal their intentions to other males, or both.

Scott Kraus and other researchers have suggested that females use SAGs as a way of selecting mates who are agile, strong, and good at holding their breath. Since SAGs have been observed in the summer even though whales give birth in the winter after a gestational period of twelve months, it is believed that most SAGs do not result in fertilization. Indeed, SAGs composed of all-females and all-males have been reported, confirming that while some SAGs are for courtship or mating practice, others may be for socializing and play.

At birth, a NARW will measure between four and five metres long. The calf will nurse from nipples that, until they are needed for nursing, are tucked into two slits on the mother's abdomen. A baby NARW will nurse up to forty times a day, consuming up to 190 litres (50 gallons) of rich milk daily. At a year old, the calf will be between nine and ten metres long and weigh about twelve thousand kilograms. This incredible growth comes at the expense of the mother. When nursing her newborn calf, a NARW mother is fasting and living on the energy stored in her blubber until she reaches northern waters and can begin to feed again.

Mothers care for and nurse their calves for about a year. During this time a mother and calf are seldom apart. Like other baby mammals, a NARW calf will spend the majority of its first few weeks eating and sleeping, with brief periods of play in between. For the first few months, the mother will keep her calf by her side so she can see it at all times.

In the late winter, mothers and calves begin the migration north to their summer feeding grounds. As the calf grows, the mother will leave it alone for longer periods of time so she can feed. The pair will call out for each other and may also slap their flippers and flukes, or breach, to signal location so they can reunite.

Whales are born tail-first. At birth, a NARW calf is between 4 and 5 metres long and weighs between 700 and 1,000 kilograms. In a month, a newborn may gain nearly 1,000 kilograms.

Females in surface-active groups make a specific sound, which scientists describe as being similar to a cow mooing, that can be heard by males at distances of up to ten kilometres or more. **(Moira Brown)**

According to Laurie Murison, director of the Grand Manan Whale and Seabird Research Station (GMWSRS), "the calls from the mothers can sometimes be heard when she is at the surface to breathe and trying to relocate her calf. The calves are vulnerable when separated from their mothers, but the Bay of Fundy may be a relatively safe place. Even though there are great white sharks, killer whales are extremely rare in the Bay. The sharks may leave the calves alone because there are many harbour porpoises and seals available."

A NARW needs to reach at least five years of age before she will give birth to her first calf. Some NARWs don't give birth until they are twenty-one years old, although the average age for a first birth is currently believed to be ten to eleven years. Scientists are unsure as to why there is such a discrepancy. It could be that researchers miss some births, or that some calves die before they can be observed and identified,

A North Atlantic right whale mother and calf. Photo taken under a Scientific Research Permit issued by the National Marine Fisheries Service/NOAA. **(New England Aquarium)**

or that there are miscarriages. Females are able to breed for thirty years or longer.

Once the calves are weaned, the mother and juvenile do not spend time together. Scientists are not sure whether the mother or the calf initiates the separation. However, it is known that the NARW is rather solitary and only spends time in the company of other whales occasionally. These whales do not have the same strong social connections common in toothed whales. When there is an abundance of food, whales will congregate. Or, as described earlier, they will form a SAG for mating, socializing, and play.

With the increase in noise in the ocean over the past decades, whale researcher Christopher W. Clark and colleagues suggest that the chances of NARWs hearing each other is only 10 percent of what it was a hundred years ago. To put that in perspective, a lone right whale may have once been able to hear another whale four hundred kilometres away. Research suggests that because NARWs frequent areas with busy ship traffic, they may be under chronic stress. In a noisy ocean, a NARW may have more difficulty using sounds to avoid danger or to communicate with other NARWs.

Mother right whales can be very protective of their calves. According to Laurie Murison of the GMWSRS, a mother right whale has been seen using her tail to push against a lobster boat in order to protect her calf.

In order to research this phenomenon, scientists use sensitive hydrophones attached to gliders that prowl the ocean for up to four months. The gliders surface every couple of hours so the data can be transmitted. When the sound of a whale is detected, researchers update the marine maps accordingly. Knowing the locations of whales, in real time, may help ships avoid areas where NARWs are present.

Once calves like this one are weaned, the mother and juvenile do not spend time together. (**Moira Brown**)

Communication

Animals, including the NARW, have the same fives senses as humans, but each has developed to a different degree. The right whale's sense of vision is used to help find food. As with other whales, their vision is keen at the low light levels found deep in the ocean. Scientists think that when a NARW spyhops, or pokes its head above the water, it may be looking to see what is on the surface close by. Based on the examination of whale brains, scientists believe the NARW's sense of smell and taste is limited. The closeness of mothers and calves and the touching that takes place in SAGs confirms that the sense of touch is important in the NARW.

Scientists think that when a NARW spyhops, or pokes its head above the water, it may be looking to see what is on the surface close by. (Laurie Murison)

You can hear NARW sounds by searching online for the terms "sound" and "North Atlantic right whale."

All whales have incredibly good hearing, so it is not surprising that the NARW makes a variety of sounds. According to the *Encyclopedia of Marine Mammals*, these sounds consist of "moans, groans, belches, and pulses." While scientists are not sure why NARWs make these sounds, they are believed to signal a threat or act as an invitation to a SAG. Mother-calf pairs also use sound to maintain contact once the calf begins to spend time out of the mother's view. A mother NARW will "whisper" to her calf to avoid being heard by nearby predators. Studies by C. W. Clark and others have found that NARWs may be able to hear each other from distances as far as 32–48 kilometres.

Switched At Birth

By studying NARW genetics, scientists have confirmed two cases of adoption in free-swimming whales. In 1987, two NARW mothers gave birth at nearly the same time and in close proximity. Then, for an unknown reason, a switch happened, and each calf was cared for by the alternate mother. This has led scientists to wonder how mothers recognize their own calves, how calves recognize their mothers, and how long it takes for the recognition system to develop.

≋ Mogul ≋

Mogul, shown here, seems to travel to wherever food is abundant, including areas where right whales are rarely sighted, such as off Iceland. (**Anderson Cabot Center at the New England Aquarium, collected under DFO Canada permit**)

After forty years of study and surveys, scientists know a great deal about right whale behaviour. Most right whales do the expected, but that is not the case with Mogul. On April 21, 2018, Mogul was seen off the Massachusetts coast. He was next sighted July 23 off the coast of Iceland. Mogul is usually seen in the typical places along the eastern coast of Canada and the US, as are his mother, Slalom, and his siblings. So why did Mogul change things up? Scientists' best guess is that Mogul is simply going where food is abundant, including the areas where right whales are rarely sighted, such as off Iceland. Mogul was born in 2008 and is #3845 in the Right Whale Catalog.

Watching Whales

People love to watch whales. Seeing a whale lift its tail completely out of the water, slap a flipper, or breach clear out of the water can make for a very exciting whale-watching trip. People began paying to watch the gray whales off San Diego, California, in the 1950s. Whale-watching for beluga and fin whales began in the St. Lawrence River in the early 1970s. By the late 1970s, once scientists realized that there were right whales in the Bay of Fundy, people began watching whales in this area too. By the 1980s, whale-watching off the east coast of the US had become big business.

Whale-watching, as a recreational and educational activity, has grown considerably in the last few decades. A large study published in 2009 estimated that 13 million people worldwide went whale-watching the previous year in 119 countries, and that number only seems to be growing.

Reputable whale-watching tour operators follow a code of ethics that prioritizes the safety of the whale. Operators are encouraged to share whale sightings with other tour boats in the area and captains are advised to move away from any whale exhibiting avoidance behaviours such as lobtailing or quickly fleeing from the presence of a boat. Tour boats should also be aware of the location of fishing gear and take steps to avoid steering whales towards these potentially dangerous areas. Most importantly, good tour operators educate the public about the conservation of whales and the need to preserve the ecosystem.

Passengers on a whale-watching tour should understand that they are at sea, observing a wild animal in its

Do the three different species of right whales "speak" the same language? Beginning in 1999 Dr. Susan E. Parks played the courtship sounds of the female Southern right whale to a group of North Atlantic right whales in the Bay of Fundy. The sounds made by the two different species of right whales seemed to be same and it was hypothesized that only males would respond to the female courtship calls. When NARWs of all genders and ages responded, scientists concluded that they were all curious and wanted to investigate a "voice" that they did not recognize.

Seeing a whale lift its tail completely out of the water can make for a very exciting whale-watching trip. **(Laurie Murison)**

natural habitat. Whale behaviour cannot be predicted and it is always a possibility that whales will not be observed on the day of the tour. It is important to remember that tour operators are not permitted to engage in behaviours that can be harmful or disruptive to any whale simply to satisfy clients eager to engage with a whale. If a boat captain manoeuvres the boat in such a way that it appears to disturb a whale, passengers are encouraged to object. The safety of the whale should be paramount. Unfortunately, included among the dangers whales face are uninformed or careless pleasure-craft operators. Boaters who do not take appropriate precautions to ensure that whales are not stressed by their actions can be charged under the Fisheries Act.

One of the dangers whales face is from uninformed or careless pleasure-craft operators who may inadvertently cause whales stress by getting too close. **(Nick Barry)**

Spyhopping, Breaching, and Lobtailing

While they are incredibly rare to spot, the NARW engages in all the expected behaviours whale-watchers seek, and is so flexible it can almost touch its fluke with its snout. It is thought that, like other whales, the NARW engages in spyhopping—keeping its head above water—so that it can have a look at what might be on the surface of the water. It is also known for lobtailing: slapping its tail fluke on the water's surface. NARWs may do this as a warning to other whales, or in an effort to keep boaters away.

While there is much speculation about why whales exhibit these behaviours, scientists don't really know why. It is assumed that they are a means to communicate with other whales. Younger whales seem to breach, lobtail, and spyhop more frequently than older whales. The behaviours may be aggressive in nature, or the whales may just be having fun!

Some popular whale-watching spots may be frequented by several different companies, with boat tours operating morning, afternoon, and evening. When done properly, keeping the well-being of the whales the number-one priority, whale-watching can convince even the most indifferent individual that whales are worthy of protection from the harm caused by human activity.

~

Although whales may seem unaffected or habituated to the frequent presence and sound of boats in their environment, scientists claim that whales are probably stressed by the constant presence of cargo ships, fishing boats, and even pleasure crafts. Such long-term stress can have a negative impact on NARW health. In fact, even scientists must apply for special permits before a research boat or a plane can get any closer than 457 metres (500 yards) from an endangered NARW in the US, or within 100 metres in Canada (200 metres if a mother/calf pair).

Scientists must apply for special permits before their research boats can get close to endangered NARWs.
(Laurie Murison)

In the summer of 2018, the Canadian government imposed new regulations to try to protect cetaceans. It is now illegal to feed whales, to try to swim with them, or to come between a mother and calf. It is considered a criminal offence to interfere with a whale. Offenders risk a penalty of between $100,000 and $500,000. People are also required to report all ship strikes or observations of entangled whales. Boats must maintain a minimum distance from whales, with the distance varying by area and species. A good rule of thumb is to ensure that boats maintain a distance of at least 500 metres from any whale. DFO encourages the public to follow this recommendation: "If you see tail, fin or spray—stay far enough away."

Anyone who spots a whale in waters off the Maritime provinces should report the sighting to: XMARWhaleSightings@dfo-mpo.gc.ca. Without approaching the whale, try to record and report important details such as species, number of whales, location, date, and time.

Chapter 4

THE PROBLEM: What Is Killing the North Atlantic Right Whale?

"There will either be drastic measures taken to save the North Atlantic right whale or a running tally to its extinction."

–Regina Asmutis-Silva, executive director, Whale and Dolphin Conservation–North America, *CBC News*

The right whale was hunted to near extinction twice. The Basque whalers practically decimated the population at the end of the 1500s. Towards the end of the 1880s commercial whaling likely reduced the population to less than 100. Humans and their activities remain the largest threat to this great whale. Indeed, half of all known North Atlantic right whale deaths can be directly linked to human interactions. The two main causes of death in right whales are ship strikes and entanglement in fishing gear.

There are other very different reasons that NARWs may be dying prematurely, and these, too, can also be related, indirectly, to humans. Increased levels of pollution in NARW habitats may be leading to more frequent and harmful algal blooms that kill fish, birds, and whales. Algal blooms, also known as red tide, are an aggregation of algae that can develop a poisonous substance referred to as lethal biotoxins. When these toxic substances are a part of the marine food web, they can cause respiratory problems in right whales. Additionally, climate change may be degrading the habitat of copepods, the main NARW food source.

Stressed-out Right Whales

NARWs are under stress, and scientists are trying to get to the bottom of it. One way scientists are attempting to learn more about NARW health is by collecting and analyzing the spray when a whale surfaces and expels air, or "blows." Imagine the challenge of trying to collect the spray from a fifteen-metre, free-swimming whale! In addition to being at precisely the right place when a whale surfaces, one has to be ready with a petri dish secured to the end of a long pole to catch the spray, just as the whale exhales. By analyzing the hormone levels in the blow, researchers can better understand the whale's reproductive capacity, metabolism, and stress level.

Another way that scientists are learning more about the health of NARWs is to analyze their feces. In 1999, veterinarian Rosalind Rolland began to collect and analyze whale feces to determine whether a whale was pregnant. Her theory was simple, and it worked on terrestrial wildlife. (And humans aren't too different. Since the 1970s, women have been urinating on test sticks to see if they are pregnant.) Using a long pole and a fine mesh net, Rolland began collecting samples. Luckily, right whale feces is easy to see, and it floats. At first, researchers simply collected samples when they saw a right whale defecate, something whales do when feeding at the surface, before they dive, and when involved in a courtship group. A few years later, researchers began to use dogs to help sniff out the whale feces. These dogs, trained like drug-sniffing dogs, react to the smell of right

One way scientists are attempting to learn more about NARW health is by collecting and analyzing the spray when a whale surfaces and expels air, or "blows." **(Laurie Murison)**

whale feces. While a human can smell the feces from a distance of 350 metres, a trained dog can catch the scent on the ocean breezes when the feces is almost 2 kilometres away!

Analysis of the feces can tell the researchers the gender of the whale and whether it is pregnant or lactating, or under stress. Chronic stress can impact a whale in the same way it affects humans. A stressed whale may be underweight, have trouble recovering when ill, be unable to get pregnant or feed efficiently, and experience changes in diving patterns. Fecal analysis is also used to detect the presence of parasites and toxins.

The continual study of NARW feces, and the information learned by its analysis, is helping to build medical and individual profiles of some of the individuals found in the Right Whale Catalog. Hopefully, it will lead to some answers on how to save this incredible species.

Stressed whales are susceptible to disease and have a reduced fertility rate. Reproductive females previously produced calves every three to five years. Today, it is more likely that a span of ten years will pass between births. Whether females are miscarrying or just not getting pregnant is unknown. What is known, however, is that there are fewer than an estimated 71 reproductive females remaining in the entire NARW population. We also know that the entire population is descended from just a few females. Some scientists have concluded that inbreeding may have led to the current low fertility rate.

The Right Whale Catalog documents a number of females who have no reported calves. The population of Southern right whales has rebounded with a birth rate that is now double that of the NARW. Many factors may be involved, but the result is the same: there are more deaths than births each year. With the current population of just over 400 whales, the math is easy. If there are no new births and 20 whales die each year, the NARW population will be extinct by the middle of this century.

Noisy Oceans

The development of offshore wind farms is adding to the sound pollution of the ocean environment. (iStock.com/shaunl)

When engines began to power ships, the noise level in the oceans began to rise. The increased number and size of ships causes more noise. Seismic exploration, the development of offshore wind farms, and naval activity in the calving grounds are all adding to the sound pollution of the ocean environment. The NARW depends on hearing to find mates. How the increase in noise is affecting these whales is uncertain, but what is known is that the ocean is one hundred times noisier than it was in 1960. Studies by scientist Susan Parks have shown that the sounds produced by right whales in the 1990s were much louder than those that right whales made in the 1970s. In a noisier ocean, NARWs now have to shout to be heard!

It's also known that whales can certainly hear ship traffic, which leads many to wonder, why don't they just get out of the way? Dr. Phil

9/11 and the Bay of Fundy Right Whales

The September 11, 2001, attacks in New York City gave scientists an unexpected chance to test how ocean noise can cause stress in right whales. Scientists from the NEAq were conducting studies in the Bay of Fundy, where they had been collecting whale feces to measure the stress levels of right whales. Samples were collected before, during, and after the attacks. During the four days when planes were grounded, there were also far fewer ships moving and this resulted in less noise in the right whale habitat. Tests showed that NARW stress levels were lower when the ocean was quieter. Once traffic returned to normal, the stress level in whales returned to the same levels as before the attacks.

Clapham, a scientist with the US government's National Oceanographic and Atmospheric Administration, and one of the world's leading experts in large whales, has concluded that there are now so many ships in the ocean that if a whale moved to avoid every ship it heard, it wouldn't have time to feed. Right whales may be habituated to ship sounds, but the way sound travels in the ocean may cause it to seem quieter at the front of a ship than behind it. After twenty minutes submerged, and with a couple strokes of a powerful tail, a right whale may surface in the wrong place: at the bow of a ship. The result is often tragic for the whale.

Busy Oceans

With the number of right whale deaths increasing and the population decreasing, mariners and scientists are working together to find ways to avoid collisions. Vessel surveys conducted between 1987 and 2002 showed that ships and NARWs were typically found in the same part of the Bay of Fundy. The ships were travelling to and from the port of Saint John, New Brunswick, also home to a large oil refinery, and moving through a prime whale

Between 1987 and 2002 ships and NARWs were typically found in the same part of the Bay of Fundy. The ships were travelling to and from the port of Saint John, New Brunswick. In 2003 the shipping lanes in the Bay of Fundy were successfully changed, which has likely saved the lives of some NARWs. **(iStock.com/bridixon)**

feeding area. A group of scientists, led by Dr. Moira Brown, now with the Canadian Whale Institute, made the case that with a small change to the shipping lanes, the bay would become safer for whales. The suggested change was based on scientific data and provided a solution that could work for big business, the transportation industry, government, and the whales. In 2003 the shipping lanes in the Bay of Fundy were successfully changed. This has resulted in many fewer whale sightings in the shipping lanes. The change has meant fewer ship strikes and has likely saved the lives of some NARWs.

Fast Ships and Slow Whales

"Speed restrictions...were particularly unappealing to mariners, in part because they were considered contrary to age-old traditions that vested sole authority for safe operation of vessels in ship captains."

–David W. Laist, *North Atlantic Right Whales: From Hunted Leviathan to Conservation Icon*

Prior to 1800, ships were powered by wind and moved at an average speed of 4 to 8 knots per hour. Once oceangoing vessels became steam-powered, their speed increased. By the mid-1800s, ships' speed had nearly doubled and ships were able to travel at more than 14 knots per hour. Today some vessels, such as container and cruise ships, can travel in excess of 20 knots.

In 1885, while travelling at a speed of 13 knots, a boat killed a whale off Nantucket, Massachusetts, one of the first recorded ship strikes off the US coast. Researcher David Laist and others found reports of at least fourteen additional fatal ship strikes over the next seventy years. By the 1950s, ships were travelling at 12 to 14 knots, and reports of whales killed by ship strikes began to accumulate. By 1970, one-third of right whale deaths were attributed to ship strikes; by 1990, that percentage increased to half. Typically, whales are killed by ships when they come in to contact with the propellers or when a ship hits a logging or surfacing whale, causing death from blunt force trauma.

≋ Shackleton ≋

"He is a great little whale that had gone through so many hardships and it was great to see that he made it." –Phillip K. Hamilton, New England Aquarium

Shackleton, shown here, defied the odds: he survived a near stranding—just as his namesake, Sir Ernest Shackleton, had done. **(Anderson Cabot Center at the New England Aquarium, collected under DFO Canada permit)**

No one knows why Shackleton swam 160 kilometres up the Delaware River to Philadelphia in December of 1994. But he survived encounters with oil tankers and a near stranding under a pier surrounded by oil booms, pilings, and pipes. Aided by many people, Shackleton was turned around and directed downriver to the sea, only to be hit by a tug boat before reaching open ocean. Shackleton was seen in the Bay of Fundy nearly two years later, showing evidence of another ship strike. He had a row of scars from contact with boat propellers.

Researchers named this whale after Antarctic explorer Sir Ernest Shackleton, who defied the odds and survived after his ship was crushed in ice, stranding him and his crew in the middle of the sea at the south pole! Shackleton is #2440 in the Right Whale Catalog. He was likely born in January of 1994 and was last seen in 2017 in Cape Cod Bay.

To try to reduce the number of whale deaths by ship strikes, a number of measures have been considered: reducing ship speed, moving shipping lanes, advising mariners of seasonal areas to be avoided, and warning ships about the presence of whales. In experimental tests, some of the sounds used in an attempt to keep whales away from ships actually led whales to swim just below the surface to investigate the noise. As this method put whales in even greater danger, it was never implemented. Speed restrictions and lane changes, where implemented, seem to have reduced NARW mortality. Extending such measures may make the ocean safer for slow-moving right whales.

Using Technology to Spot Whales

Scientists and others have been working on more effective ways to try to reduce ship strikes. Aerial surveys alert ships when right whales are observed nearby. This Early Warning System (EWS) was first implemented in the late 1980s off the coasts of Florida and Georgia and was later extended to the waters off New England. In the beginning of the EWS, air crews reported whale sightings to harbour controllers, who then relayed the information to vessels in the area. Now, thanks to improvements in technology, near real-time NARW sightings are available to all mariners.

There is one obvious problem with this system, however: whales spend most of their lives under water, where they can't be easily observed. At night and in heavy fog there is no ability to see and report whale presence. It is estimated that fewer than half of the whales in an area can be observed from a plane. Additionally, it takes time and a fair distance to change the course of a large, fast-moving ship. Even with warnings that whales are close by, collisions between ships and whales still happen.

Whales and Fishers

No fisher wants to be responsible for entangling a NARW. Most fishers understand the problem and want to do what they can do to help stop the leading cause of deaths in right whales. With 83 percent of all NARWs entangled at least once, and more than half entangled more than once, fishers know this has to change.

Entanglement also means loss of gear and a loss of potential catch for the fisher. The stronger ropes developed in the 1990s reduce the amount of lost gear and are good for the fishing industry. But stronger gear keeps whales entangled for a longer period. Tight ropes cut into skin and cause infection. Prolonged infection weakens the animal, leading to weight loss and increased susceptibility to disease. Some NARW necropsies have shown that fishing rope can become so tight, it penetrates to the bone.

Entanglement means loss of gear and a loss of potential catch for fishers. The stronger ropes developed in the 1990s reduce the amount of lost gear and are good for the fishing industry, but stronger gear keeps whales entangled for a longer period. (iStock.com/shaunl)

International Whaling Commission

The International Whaling Commission (IWC) was established in 1948, as a part of the International Convention for the Regulation of Whaling, to manage commercial whaling. The IWC was charged with setting limits on the numbers of whales that could be caught each year. Smithsonian scientist Nick Pyenson said, "In theory, the IWC was meant to regulate the killing of whales; in practice, the IWC functioned more like an international hunting club."

Canada withdrew from the IWC in 1982, arguing that there was a lack of scientific evidence to justify the moratorium on commercial whaling. This action was criticized by anti-whaling groups even though Canada had banned commercial whaling in 1972.

By 1986 the IWC put a moratorium on all commercial whaling. Many countries objected. Iceland, Norway, and Russia have ignored the ban and have created their own quotas for a commercial whale hunt. Japan issues a scientific permit that allows whales to be killed as part of the country's cetacean research. The meat from whales caught with this scientific permit is sold under the argument that it would be a waste to not consume it. Many anti-whaling groups say the scientific permits are just a way to condone commercial whaling in Japan.

In 2018 the IWC rejected a proposal from Japan, which was supported by twenty-seven other countries, including Norway and Iceland, to resume commercial whaling. These countries continue to hunt and kill whales.

Mariners, Fishers, and Government Regulation

In the US, when at least 3 whales have been spotted within a 75 square–nautical mile area, mariners are asked to slow down. This voluntary slowdown lasts for fifteen days. In Canada, in the summer of 2018, fishing areas were closed for fifteen days whenever a single NARW was seen. The time period could be extended if the whale remained in the closed area.

Fishers, their families, and others who depend on the fishery for their livelihoods, objected to these measures. They felt that the closures were too long and covered too large an area. The closures applied to both the lobster and crab fisheries, which fishers argued did not make sense, as lobster traps are set close to shore and are therefore not a threat to NARWs. Fishers felt that drastic measures were being implemented without sufficient cause. They were upset that government officials, who don't spend time on the water, and who may be influenced by environmental lobby groups, were making the decisions. Tensions between fishers and the Canadian government ran high that summer. Some in the fishing community felt the government was favouring whales over people.

A North Atlantic right whale lifts its tail flukes in preparation for a deep dive. **(Laurie Murison)**

For the 2019 fishing season, changes have been made. The boundaries of the snow crab closure were changed and the closed area made smaller, reflecting the location of right whales during the 2018 fishing season. Lobster fishing areas in less than twenty fathoms of water were not subject to a static closure. Dynamic measures were the same as the previous year. Only time will tell if making annual adjustments to the boundaries based on whale sightings from the previous fishing season is the right decision when it comes to protecting the NARW.

Chapter 5

SAVING WHALES:
Who Is Helping and How?

"What hope is there for the North Atlantic right whale? Scientists, conservationists, governments, and consumers are giving right whales a voice. Mariners and fishers are changing their ways on the water to give right whales room to live and hopefully thrive, but not without cost and frustration. Together, we strive to achieve a restoration challenge of great magnitude for a species that has shown incredible resilience despite centuries of setbacks from whaling, and then decades of unintentional human-related mortality from fishing and shipping."

–Dr. Moira Brown, Canadian Whale Institute

In the previous chapters, you read about some of the efforts by scientists and research organizations to save the North Atlantic right whale. Here is a look at what fishers, individuals, conservation groups, and governments are doing to keep the North Atlantic right whale from disappearing.

Fishing Equipment

Scientists have determined that at least 83 percent of all NARWs have been entangled in fishing gear. Entanglement can weaken a NARW and lead to premature death. Fishers don't want to be responsible for injuring or killing whales. What can be done to fishing gear that will reduce the impact on whales and will work for the fishing industry?

Rope Entanglement

> "If people saw this [entanglement] on a cat or dog, they would be outraged and not allow it to happen."
>
> —New England Aquarium scientist, Philip K. Hamilton, *Deep Trouble* podcast

Fishing rope is much stronger now than it was prior to the 1990s. This heavy rope is used in aquaculture operations. (Ken Boehner)

Fishing rope is much stronger now than it was prior to the 1990s. This means that less gear is lost, and this saves time and money for fishers. But stronger ropes last longer and are much more difficult for entangled whales to shed. Efforts are underway to test gear with a built-in weak link, or connector, so an entangled whale may have a better chance of shedding the gear. This may be good for the entangled whale, but could mean more lost gear for fishers and more derelict gear and rope to entangle another whale. Will this compromise be accepted in the fishing industry?

To try to reduce the amount of rope in the water, an acoustic-release mechanism is being tested. Here's how it works: Traditional traps sit on the bottom of the ocean and are connected by rope to a buoy that floats at the surface. The buoy marks the trap's location and owner. Ropes are used to pull the gear back to the surface so traps can be emptied.

With acoustic-release traps, the buoy, the rope, and a retrieval mechanism stay with the trap on the ocean floor. When it is time to empty the trap, the fisher sends a signal to the acoustic-release mechanism on the trap, causing the buoy and the attached rope to float to the surface. Then the rope is used to pull up the trap.

Whales can become entangled in the ropes beneath buoys and markers like these. (Ken Boehner)

While this method would be much safer for whales, and fishers are eager to test out the technology, it is expensive to retrofit traditional traps: it can cost up to $1,000 per trap outfitted with the acoustic-release mechanism. Individual lobster fishers can have as many as 300 traps, while crab fishers may have 150. There is much debate about who should pay the cost for making this change. Should the government cover the entire cost, or is it the responsibility of individual fishers and, ultimately, consumers? Another potential issue with this system is that, with the buoys on the ocean floor, it may be more difficult for fishers and DFO fisheries enforcement to see where others have set traps.

One company is working to develop an acoustic-release mechanism that would reduce the amount of rope used with traps, making it less likely that whales become entangled. (Ashored Innovations)

Individual lobster fishers can have as many as 300 traps; it can cost up to $1,000 per trap to be outfitted with an acoustic-release mechanism. **(Ken Boehner)**

Another approach to having less rope in the water is to reduce the number of lines (ropes) attached to lobster and crab traps. Traditional traps have one line to one buoy at the surface. Fishers are attaching forty to fifty traps together at the bottom with only two lines of rope going up through the water column to the surface. This is known as the "trawl." So instead of having three hundred lines of rope in the water with one line for each trap, six trawls with fifty traps will only have twelve lines (one on each end of the trawl) floating in the water column. By doing this, fishers hugely reduce the amount of rope used, making a fishing area somewhat safer for whales.

Ghost Gear

In an effort to reduce the danger to marine mammals caused by lost fishing gear, Canada's federal government requires that fishers report all lost gear. But fishers have been trying to

Derelict fishing gear can sometimes be repurposed, as these old lobster traps have been. **(Ken Boehner)**

find and remove "ghost gear" for years. Derelict gear collects and forms giant snarls that drift and snag on even more gear. Locally, the Fundy North Fishermen's Association is working to actively seek out and collect ghost gear. Thankfully, it's not simply going into the landfill—it is being repurposed. Old rope is being made into floor mats, and broken lobster traps are being filled with stones to form the bases of retaining walls.

One great example of a marine recycling initiative is the Huntsman Marine Science Centre in Saint Andrews,

This used fishing rope collection bin, on the wharf at Lord's Cove on Deer Island, New Brunswick, is popular with local fishers. (**Huntsman Marine Science Centre**)

Jaclyn Walker, outreach coordinator at the Huntsman Marine Science Centre in Saint Andrews, New Brunswick, is shown here with some of the collected rope. (**Huntsman Marine Science Centre**)

New Brunswick, which has placed bins at several wharves in southwestern New Brunswick where fishers can deposit used rope. Thousands of kilograms of the collected rope have gone to a nearby recycling facility and some is used in programming at the centre, where visitors can learn how to weave the rope into a decorative mat.

New Boat Design

Construction Navale Atlantique, a shipbuilding company in New Brunswick, is producing crab and lobster fishing boats that may be safer for NARWs. The design comes from France, where these boats are used by law enforcement and rescue agencies. More of the boat is above the

Used fishing rope can be repurposed into decorative items like these. (**Huntsman Marine Science Centre**)

Marine Stewardship Council

The Marine Stewardship Council (MSC) is a non-profit organization based in London, England, that was established in 1996 by the multinational food and consumer goods corporation Unilever and the World Wide Fund for Nature or WWF (formerly the World Wildlife Fund) to set standards for sustainable fisheries. In order to be sustainable, fish harvesters have to leave enough stock in the ocean to enable it to flourish, reduce their impact on the ecosystem, practice effective fisheries management, and quickly adapt to changes necessary to ensure that future generations can fish and enjoy seafood. Fisheries that the MSC deems sustainable can pay a royalty to for the right to use the MSC ecolabel on their products.

Some people have questioned this, accusing the MSC program of a conflict of interest. The MSC was said to have increased its income by permitting the use of its ecolabel for some seafood products with questionable sustainability.

In 2017 the MSC certified the Gulf of St. Lawrence snow crab fishery as sustainable. This designation means that the seafood can be sold with the MSC ecolabel. The certification was suspended in early 2018 as the snow crab fishery was linked to the entanglement of five and the deaths of three NARWs in 2017. If the fishery is able to make changes to ensure sustainability, certification may be re-established after the MSC completes its re-evaluation. The results are expected in 2020.

In 2018 the Government of Canada temporarily closed some fisheries in Atlantic Canada over concerns that all Canadian fisheries were in danger of completely losing their MSC certification if more was not done to protect the NARW.

water line than in traditional fishing boats. This makes the boat more stable and fuel efficient. With less of the boat in the water, it is believed this type of vessel will be less dangerous to whales.

"If we don't take robust, science-based, coherent measures to protect these highly endangered North Atlantic right whales, we're really playing Russian roulette with the entire future of the Canadian fish and seafood industry."

–Dominic LeBlanc, Federal Fisheries Minister

To help locate NARWs, Drs. Kimberley Davies and Chris Taggart of Dalhousie University in Halifax have developed the Whales, Habitat and Listening Experiment, or WHaLE project. Underwater gliders that resemble small planes travel through the waters of Atlantic Canada, listening for whale sounds and reporting this data back to researchers. The data from the gliders is combined with information from visual surveillance on WhaleMap, a project undertaken by the Dalhousie University–based Marine Environmental Observation, Prediction and Response Network (MEOPAR), an independent not-for-profit that focuses on human impacts on the marine environment. A map showing the locations of NARWs can assist mariners in plotting a course that may help them avoid a fatal ship strike. According to the WhaleMap website, "successful conservation relies on finding these whales—an extraordinarily difficult task given limited resources and a vast ocean."

Rescuing Whales in Newfoundland

The first person to rescue a free-swimming whale off the coast of Newfoundland was Jon Lien, who, at the time, was teaching at Memorial University of Newfoundland and a friend to many local fishers. In 1978 he was called by a fisher who had a humpback whale caught in his cod nets. Lien freed the whale and went on to establish a whale-release program called Tangly Whales. In 2001 it became known as Whale Release and Strandings. Thanks to their work, thousands of whales have been saved in waters off Newfoundland.

The WHaLE project also measures the quantity of copepods in the area. If copepods are plentiful, there are likely to be NARWs too. Knowing the locations of concentrations of NARW food will help guide marine management decisions. To predict where a NARW will be, follow the copepods. To lessen ship strikes and entanglements and make an area safer for whales, governments can plan to close areas of the ocean when there is, or is likely to be, a dense aggregation of copepods. According to Dr. Kim Davies: "When you are trying to decide where a closed-off area should be, it should encompass not only where you are seeing whales today, but where you might expect them to be over longer time and space scales."

Scientists remain hopeful that the use of technology, and efforts such as the WHaLE project, will ultimately help reduce the human impact on NARWs.

Governmental Approach

To try to reduce human impacts on NARWs, the Government of Canada has developed a "tackle box approach." The tackle box, or tool chest, includes actions that can be implemented as needed: less rope in the water, better tracking of fishing gear, reporting lost gear, reporting of interaction between fishers and whales, closing fishing areas, exploring new technology and fishing methods, more surveillance, and possible changes to regulations. In the summer of 2018 the government began implementing closures of fishing grounds. In the Gulf of St. Lawrence and the two critical habitat areas (Grand Manan and Roseway Basin), a fisheries area can be closed for a minimum of fifteen days on the basis of a single NARW sighting. This dynamic closure can be extended for another fifteen days from the date of the most recent NARW sighting.

Volunteer Whale Rescuers

The Campobello Whale Rescue Team (CWRT) was co-founded in 2002 by Joe Howlett, a former Coast Guard employee who later joined a whale-watching tour company, and Captain Mackie Greene. A biologist, a retired Fisheries and Oceans Canada (DFO) staffer, fishers, and other mariners make up the volunteer whale-rescue team. Team members often give up paying work to participate in a rescue mission. They have undergone extensive training in rescue techniques and safety measures and have devised many of the tools used for this very specialized work. Howlett, in particular, had a reputation for being very safety conscious and for wishing to give back to the ocean that provided him with his livelihood.

In the summer of 2017, after 7 whales were found dead, the CWRT received a call to help save a badly entangled whale. Volunteer Joe Howlett and NEAq researcher Phil Hamilton were in the area and answered the call. They had planned to spend the day gathering zooplankton samples and surveying for NARWs. When they eventually got to the whale, they could see how badly entangled it was. Rope was wrapped around its body, flippers, and through its mouth. On the first try, Howlett was able to cut one line before the whale escaped. On the second approach, Howlett was able to cut another line. This time, when the whale escaped, it flipped its huge tail flukes and struck Howlett.

Author Joann Hamilton-Barry with Captain Mackie Greene of the Campobello Whale Rescue Team. **(Nick Barry)**

The Canadian Whale Institute (CWI) was established in 1997 to increase awareness of the NARW, to conduct research, to conserve marine mammals, and to educate both industry and the public. This group, under the leadership of Dr. Moira Brown, was instrumental in moving shipping lanes in the Bay of Fundy, making the area safer for NARWs. The Campobello Whale Rescue Team (CWRT) became a part of the CWI in 2014.

Author Joann Hamilton-Barry spots a whale while on Captain Mackie Greene's tour boat. **(Nick Barry)**

Joe Howlett, who co-founded the Campobello Whale Rescue Team, attempts to disentangle right whale #4057, nicknamed FDR. (**Jerry Conway/Campobello Whale Rescue Team**)

The force was equivalent to being hit by a dump truck. Phil Hamilton performed CPR for the ninety minutes it took to return to shore, where emergency medical personnel pronounced Joe Howlett deceased.

Joe Howlett, fifty-nine years old, was a husband, father, friend, fisher, and whale rescuer. In the summer before his death on July 10, 2017, he had already rescued 2 whales. That same summer saw the deaths of 17 North Atlantic right whales. The whale he rescued on the day of his death was seen swimming, free of ropes, on July 29, 2017.

After Howlett's death, the DFO suspended all whale rescues. In the summer of 2018, new measures aimed at protecting the safety of whale rescuers were announced and whale rescues resumed. On July 14, 2018, the CWRT rescued an entangled humpback calf, their first rescue since the death of their co-founder the previous summer.

Whale #3843

NARW #3843 is a nine-year-old male, offspring of #1243. This Bay of Fundy whale has been spotted almost every year since it was born in 2007. In June of 2018, #3843 was spotted swimming freely in the Gulf of St. Lawrence. On July 30, 2018, the whale was spotted by the Grand Manan Whale and Seabird Research Station (GMWSRS) dragging two buoys and rope. The CWRT was called but, due to boat mechanical problems, couldn't respond. Given the whale's obvious and severe deterioration since the June sighting, officials assumed that #3843 might only survive for a few more months. On August 5, 2018, after a week of searching for the whale, the GMWSRS team again found the whale and reported it. The CWRT was called and was able to disentangle the whale within about ninety minutes. Whale #3843 was the second rescue and the first right whale rescued by the Campobello Whale Rescue Team since the death of Joe Howlett in the summer of 2017.

~

While the DFO is responsible for the protection of the NARW and other endangered marine species, Maritime DFO staff only respond to whale strandings—they do not attempt to disentangle whales. The DFO will provide support to permitted whale rescue groups. (Things are different on the west coast of Canada, as the DFO has the sole responsibility for cutting lines on entangled whales.) Originally, the DFO loaned the Campobello Whale Rescue Team (CWRT) two used boats and gave the volunteer group the responsibility for whale disentanglement and a small grant to cover the costs of insuring the vessels and some equipment. The volunteers in the CWRT counted on donations from individuals and other concerned stakeholders, such as the International Fund for Animal Welfare, to help cover the cost of gas and maintenance to keep the boats running.

MARS: Response, Research, Education

Established in 1990, and originally known as the Nova Scotia Stranding Network, the Marine Animal Response Society (MARS) is dedicated to the conservation of marine mammals in the Maritimes. MARS staff responds to calls about injured, entangled, or stranded whales and will co-ordinate efforts to save the marine animal. When rescue isn't possible, the goal of MARS is to understand the cause of death and try to prevent similar events in the future. MARS played a lead role in coordinating the necropsies of some of the NARWs that died in Maritime waters in the summer of 2017.

Go to marineanimals.ca to learn more about MARS. If you see a stranded or injured marine mammal in the Maritimes, call MARS at 1-866-567-6277.

Currently, the CWRT is permitted by DFO to disentangle whales in the Maritimes and in the Gulf and Quebec regions. They also provide training sessions with fishers and others to help fill the response gap in the Gulf of St. Lawrence.

What to do if you see an entangled whale:

» Contact the Canadian Coast Guard or the Marine Animal Response Society (MARS).

» Keep your eyes on the whale until help arrives.

» If you can't stay, try to get another boat to keep the whale under observation. Once a whale disappears, it is not usually relocated the same day.

» Don't try to cut any trailing lines as these will be used by the disentanglement team to try to free the whale.

Chapter 6

FUTURE:

What Is the Future of the North Atlantic Right Whale & What Can We Do to Help?

"That any North Atlantic right whales survived to see the twentieth century is something of a miracle."

–David W. Laist, *North Atlantic Right Whales: From Hunted Leviathan to Conservation Icon*

"To do better, it is going to take a lot of collaboration between everybody involved."

–Amy Knowlton, research scientist, New England Aquarium, *Cape Cod Times*

Scientists have speculated that inbreeding and a lack of genetic diversity could be causing low birth rates in the NARW. A declining food supply, pollution in the food supply, disease, and habitat loss may also be preventing the population from increasing. Climate change and overfishing that reduce biodiversity have altered NARW habitats. Noisier oceans and naval and seismic activity are affecting right whales' ability to communicate, and ultimately to find food. The one thing that may work in favour of the NARW is that the species has a long lifespan, potentially providing it time to recover.

On another hopeful note, the current population size of the NARW may have been underestimated. Genetic research on the NARW has shown that only 45 percent of the known population has been fathered by known males. Who fathered the rest of the whales? Where are these absent whales? Are they travelling in search of food or a mate? Some research indicates that there may be more NARWs out there, but none have yet been found in areas where researchers have focused their efforts. Sadly, it is also possible that the population estimate of 411 NARWs, according to the North Atlantic Right Whale Consortium's 2018 report card, is an overestimate. Hopefully, the long lifespan and the ability of the NARW to travel huge distances will help it survive. But we can't count on those factors alone.

Many are working to change the conditions that are harmful to the NARW. Given current birth and mortality rates, the present population of about 400 whales is not sustainable. If current circumstances do not change, experts predict that the NARW will be extinct as early as 2040. For the NARW to recover, Canadian scientists are working "to achieve an increasing trend in population abundance over three generations," according to the Canadian Right Whale Recovery Plan released in 2009. In the US recovery plan in 2005, the country's scientists set a goal of a population increase to 1,200 individuals. Are these goals realistic, or even possible? While experts are not certain of pre-exploitation population size, estimates range, suggesting that around 1000 BCE there may have been as few as 2,000 or as many as 10,000 NARWs. Scientists state that if we can prevent the deaths of just 2 breeding females each year, the NARW population has a chance of recovering.

Was the summer of 2017, when 17 right whales were killed, just a bad summer to be a right whale, or was it a signal that the end is near for this great whale? Is it possible that large numbers of right whales have died in previous summers and their bodies were not found, their deaths left unrecorded? Scientists worry that at least 20 whales die each year and simply that more bodies were found in 2017 than in previous summers. It is also possible that more than 17 right whales died in 2017 and their bodies were not found. In 2016 scientists were optimistic that the outlook for the right whale was improving, but this is no longer the case. Scientists fear that human-caused mortality is outpacing reproduction and current recovery efforts. Can whales adapt to survive in an ocean environment that is, itself, undergoing great changes? Can humanity do what needs to be done in time to save the NARW?

≋ Admiral ≋

Admiral is one of the largest of all of the NARWs listed in the Right Whale Catalog. She was first observed in 1979, before work on the catalog actually began. Ultrasound testing has shown that her blubber is the thickest of all of the NARWs that have been tested. She has been seen participating in SAGs, but researchers have never seen her with a calf. Admiral is also the only NARW that has been observed standing on her head, with her tail in the air. Southern right whales have been known to stand on their heads and be blown downwind, an activity known as "sailing," but no other NARW has been seen doing this. Scars on her body indicate that she had been badly entangled. Scientists now assume that Admiral is dead, since she has not been seen since 2007, in the Bay of Fundy. Admiral is #1027 in the Right Whale Catalog.

Changes Are Needed

Nick Pyenson, Smithsonian scientist and author of the book *Spying on Whales*, suggests that for the NARW to survive, it should not be picky about what it eats. But the NARW has evolved to survive by eating only copepods. What else could it eat? Will the NARW have to move to another part of the ocean with more copepods in order to survive?

Pyenson also recommends that whales "stay global" by inhabiting all parts of their ocean and expanding their gene pool as much as possible. Are some whales already doing this? Will the NARWs that don't frequent the usual summer feeding areas help to save the population? Feeding farther away from fishing areas and shipping lanes will certainly lessen the chance of human impact. Can these rural whales lead the urban or Fundy whales to a more remote, and possibly safer, part of the Atlantic Ocean? Are there aggregations of copepods there that can sustain the species? Are some NARWs exchanging long established migration patterns, calving grounds, and feeding areas for distant locations?

Some species of whales have demonstrated the ability to learn and share knowledge that may help to ensure survival. Humpback whale songs change over time and are thought to be a part of their mating rituals. Can the NARW learn and change to meet the challenges in today's ocean? Some scientists believe that it is not the responsibility of the NARW to change. Humans caused the problems that are killing the NARW, so shouldn't it be our responsibility to change?

While the future may look bleak for the NARW, many scientists feel that the ability of whales like Mogul (see page 45) to find new feeding grounds thousands of kilometres outside of normal range, or the reproductive prowess of Kleenex (see page 82) means that there is hope for the species.

Plastic Lasts Forever

A survey of harbours in Newfoundland showed that they contain everything from fridges and barbecues to bicycles, old toilets, and vinyl siding. What concerns researchers most is that there is more and more garbage every year.

Only a very small portion of plastic packaging is recycled. Much of the plastic discarded every day is from single-use items such as water bottles, grocery bags, and straws. A grocery bag may last from ten to one hundred years, a chip bag for 350 years, and a plastic water bottle for 450 to 1,000 years. But plastics don't actually degrade, they just break into smaller and smaller pieces. A shocking amount of plastic is ending up in our oceans, killing birds, fish, and marine mammals. It is estimated that there will be more plastic mass in the ocean than fish mass by 2050.

A shocking amount of plastic is ending up in our oceans, killing birds, fish, and marine mammals.
(Nick Barry)

Plastics in the ocean are being drawn into five different gyres, or vortexes, including one in the North Atlantic. The garbage pile in the Pacific Ocean is three times the size of France.

Small steps by many individuals can make a big difference. Here are a few everyday ways you can help:

» Remember to bring a reusable bag when shopping.

» Pack your lunch in reusable containers and bring your own cutlery to fast food restaurants.

» Patronize coffee shops that encourage you to bring your own mug. Reusing is better for the environment than recycling.

» Avoid helium baloons and carry a reusable water bottle; this can greatly reduce the amount of plastic that ends up in the ocean.

» Lead by example. Picking up plastic at the beach serves as a model to others.

Some people are doing even more than reducing their use of plastics or picking up plastics discarded by others. One recent example is a young Newfoundland entrepreneur who has turned his love of recycling into a clothing line: Seaside Apparel. Trevor Bessette uses fabric made from recycled plastic bottles and cotton fabric scraps to make hoodies and T-shirts and donates a portion of his profits for local activities, such as beach clean-ups, around St. John's. Keeping single-use plastics out of the ocean helps to provide a safer habitat for all sea creatures, including right whales.

Some individuals are leading campaigns to end the use of plastic shopping bags in their communities. Governments are listening, and many provinces are close to banning single-use bags. Elementary school children are lobbying school administrators to ban straws from school milk programs, and large companies are moving from plastic to compostable straws.

Sea the Right

Ally Stewart, a student at North and South Esk Regional High School in Sunny Corner, NB, sports a T-shirt created by Sea the Right. Money raised goes toward NARW conservation. **(Sea the Right)**

In May 2018, students from Sunny Corner, New Brunswick, used a class assignment challenging them to do something to change the world to raise awareness about the North Atlantic right whale. Paige Matchett and Ashley White created a line of T-shirts and hoodies called Sea the Right with a logo that features a crashing wave and whale flukes, with all profits from sales going toward NARW conservation. In just over four months they were able to donate over $2,000 to the Canadian Whale Institute, based on Campobello Island, New Brunswick.

The plastic rings that hold six-packs of cans together have been causing problems for birds, fish, and marine mammals of all sizes. Disturbing photos of turtles and other wildlife caught in these discarded rings have been widely circulated. Enterprising companies are developing strong alternatives made of material that will degrade in less than a year.

Can you make changes that will reduce plastic waste? It will benefit every creature living on this planet. Do it for yourself, your community, for future generations—and for the North Atlantic right whale.

How Else Can We Help?

People who are concerned about the North Atlantic right whale and want to do more can educate themselves in a few different ways: visiting museums featuring marine mammals (see pages 84–89 for a list of places to visit in Atlantic Canada), reading books like this one, and going online to research the work of those trying to raise awareness about the possible fate of this whale.

Adopt a Whale, or Two

Author Joann Hamilton-Barry stands by the massive whale jawbones at the entrance to the Grand Manan Whale and Seabird Research Station. (Nick Barry)

When you adopt one whale, or even a family of North Atlantic right whales, your donation helps fund research, conservation, and education efforts. Check out the section on the Grand Manan Whale and Seabird Research Station website to learn more about some of the NARWs that are up for adoption.

www.AdoptRightWhales.ca

Once informed, the next step is action. Taking time to write to politicians to express your views can impact decisions about whale management and ocean conservation. Donations to research groups, both large and small, can also make a huge difference. Many small and not-for-profit groups count on financial support from the public to fund research and to cover the costs associated with fieldwork. When gift-giving, instead of giving a trinket to the person who has everything, consider adopting a whale in their name.

Adults can help a child interested in whales by taking them to the library to find books or videos. Investigate what happens at a whale camp (see sidebar below for more), where future scientists can get hands-on experience working with educators and scientists. Instead of hosting a traditional birthday party, make it all about whales and encourage the gift of donations to conservation organizations rather than presents.

Whale Camps

Budding marine biologists can immerse themselves in the study of whales at a few locations in Atlantic Canada.

Saint Mary's University has partnered with the Canadian Whale Institute to offer a ten-day Marine Mammal Summer Camp that begins and ends in Halifax, with campers spending four days on Campobello Island.

The Fundy Marine Science Institute offers Whale Camp, an American-based program offered on Grand Manan that benefits from the expertise of the GMWSRS staff.

The Huntsman Marine Science Centre in Saint Andrews, New Brunswick, offers day programs, summer camps, field courses, and tours with a focus on active stewardship of the marine environment.

For more information, visit the following links:
- Marine Mammal Summer Camp: smu.ca/academics/ science-marine-mammal-summer-camp
- Fundy Marine Science Institute: whalecamp.com
- Huntsman Marine Science Centre: huntsmanmarine.ca

Can the North Atlantic Right Whale Survive?

"If we can't save the largest, most charismatic species on Earth, what does that mean for the rest? What does it say about us?"

–Nick Hawkins, biologist and conservation photographer

There is a groundswell of support from people all over the world who want to help ensure the NARW does not disappear forever. Scientists have identified the many threats to the NARW and the changes that must be made if the species is to survive. Technical experts are taking up the challenge and innovative solutions are being tested. Fishers do not want to see right whales caught in their gear, and many in the fishery are beginning to follow a voluntary code of conduct acknowledging that they share the ocean with endangered whales. They are learning about whales, doing what they can to make their fishing practices safer for whales, and helping to test new gear.

Kleenex

Kleenex was first seen in 1977 and is one of the most productive of all known NARWs. She is the mother of 8 calves, grandmother of 9, and has 6 great-grand calves, making her responsible for nearly 5 percent of the entire NARW population. Kleenex got her name because one of her calves had callosities shaped to look like a child with a runny nose. This calf is known to some as "Drippy Nose" but is called Sonnet in the Right Whale Catalog.

In 2014, Kleenex was observed caught in fishing gear and it appears that she has been entangled in these ropes since then. Thick, yellow fishing rope is wrapped around her mouth and across her blow hole. While the line is not tight, it is assumed to have prevented Kleenex from breeding. In April 2018, attempts were made to disentangle Kleenex. The effort was made more difficult because Kleenex did not have any trailing ropes that could be used to help in the disentanglement. Thankfully, rescuers were able to nick one of the ropes encircling her body before she disappeared underwater. It is hoped that with the rope somewhat weakened, Kleenex may be able to shed the rope on her own.

As a result of the long-term entanglement, Kleenex is very thin and her health is declining. Kleenex has been called a "rock star" by staff at the New England Aquarium because she is one of the top six reproductive females in the known NARW population. She is #1142 in the Right Whale Catalog.

Mariners also realize that industry changes are needed so whales are not injured or killed by coming into contact with ships. Researchers and entrepreneurs are developing products and technologies that will help. Educators are challenging their students to come up with solutions to prevent the disappearance of the NARW—and, as we've seen, students are taking up the challenge. Elementary school students are demanding changes to reduce the use of single-use plastics in their schools. High school students are developing products to raise awareness and donate the proceeds to help with research.

University students and start-ups are developing innovative solutions to help stop entanglements and ship strikes.

In New Brunswick, crab-fishing boats are being redesigned to pose less danger to whales. Modifications for fishing gear are being developed and tested to minimize the amount of rope in the water to reduce entanglements. Industry and scientists have worked together to move shipping lanes from areas where NARWs congregate, making some areas safer for the NARW. Individuals can pick up garbage on a beach and donate funds to aid research and rescue efforts.

The threats to the NARW are many, but we can all be a part of the solution. The time is now. Passivity and inaction are not an option if the North Atlantic right whale is to survive.

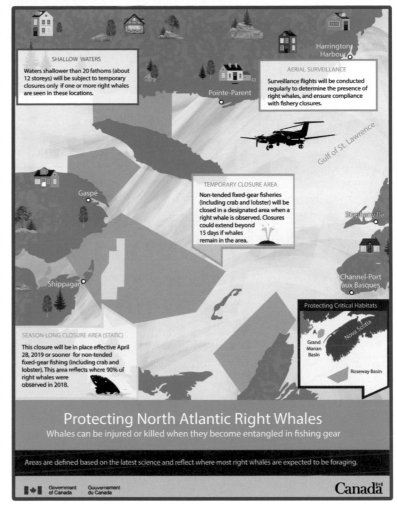

This infographic depicts some of the measures that are being taken to protect the North Atlantic right whale along Canada's east coast. **(Fisheries and Oceans Canada. Reproduced with the permission of © Her Majesty the Queen in Right of Canada, 2019)**

WHERE TO LEARN MORE ABOUT NORTH ATLANTIC RIGHT WHALES

New Brunswick

New Brunswick Museum (Saint John)

nbm-mnb.ca

The New Brunswick Museum's exhibition centre is located in the centre of uptown Saint John in the Market Square complex, also home to the oldest and best public library in Canada (but having worked there for thirty-plus years, I may be a bit biased). The museum's Hall of Great Whales features a life-size replica and the skeleton of Delilah, a right whale killed in the Bay of Fundy. (See pages 9–10 for details about Delilah.) You can learn about the powerful Bay of Fundy tides and the many other whales who make their home there, and see specimens of tiny copepods. A visit to this exhibit is an excellent way to learn about whales before going whale-watching. Visit their website to learn more.

The New Brunswick Museum in Saint John, New Brunswick, houses one of the largest marine mammal collections in the country. The museum's Hall of Great Whales features the skeleton of Delilah. (New Brunswick Museum photograph/photographie, Hall of Great Whales Gallery, Exhibition Centre, New Brunswick Museum, Market Square, Saint John, New Brunswick, 2016, digital image, NBM-F41-177)

The Grand Manan Whale and Seabird Research Station (Grand Manan Island)

gmwsrs.org

This research centre is located a short distance from the ferry landing on Grand Manan Island. Established by Dr. David Gaskin in 1981, it is dedicated to researching threatened and endangered marine mammals and seabirds of the Bay of Fundy and educating the public about their plight. The small museum is full of specimens, including baleen, copepods, and the bones from several types of whales. The gift shop has a wide selection of books and local crafts. Staff of the GMWSRS often serve as consultants to help ensure that local craftspeople capture important details in their wood carvings and other crafts featuring the right whale.

The Marine Life Interpretation Centre (Campobello Island)

canadianwhaleinstitute.ca

This centre educates visitors on biology, research, and conservation of the NARW through exhibits and on-site interpretation. Getting there can be an adventure, as it requires either two ferry rides or crossing two international borders. If the ferry is running, you sail directly from Deer Island, New Brunswick, after taking a short ferry ride from Letete, New Brunswick. If the Campobello ferry isn't running, you will need your passport. Even though Campobello Island is part of New Brunswick, it is linked to the state of Maine by a bridge. To get to the island by car, you have to cross the international border between New Brunswick and the state of Maine at St. Stephen. After clearing US customs in Calais, Maine, you'll drive about forty-five minutes through the state of Maine. At Lubec, Maine, you'll cross back into Canada on the international bridge linking Campobello to the mainland, where you need to clear Canadian customs. The Centre is a very short drive from the foot of the bridge.

This interpretation centre has been in operation since 2013 and is a partnership between the Canadian Whale Institute and the Roosevelt Campobello International Park. From the centre you may see grey seals playing in the harbour overlooking the town of Lubec, Maine, and the octagonal Mulholland Lighthouse. Once you are here, you'll have a choice of whale-watching trips. You are likely to see a minke or fin whale and can learn a great deal about all Bay of Fundy whales from the knowledgeable crew. On the drive back to Canada, you may catch a glimpse of the Passamaquoddy Bay and the town of Saint Andrews.

The Huntsman Marine Science Centre and Fundy Discovery Aquarium (Saint Andrews)

huntsmanmarine.ca

This "not-for-profit research and science-based teaching institution" is located in the town of Saint Andrews. At the aquarium you can get up close to the playful harbour seals, learn about seahorses, and hold a sea cucumber or starfish at the giant touch tank. The centre offers interpretive tours, scavenger hunts, films, beach walks, and more. The active marine biology research facility has its own research vessel, is the home of the Atlantic Reference Centre, and hosts visiting scientists. People of all ages can take part in workshops, sign up for weeklong courses, plan a sleepover at the Aquarium, or visit the café and shop.

When in Saint Andrews, you can view a spectacular stone sculpture of a right whale at the Kingsbrae Garden.

Kingsbrae Garden in Saint Andrews, New Brunswick, is home to this spectacular stone sculpture of a right whale. **(Debra Hamilton)**

Nova Scotia

Museum of Natural History (Halifax)

naturalhistory.novascotia.ca

At this Halifax museum, not far from the famous Public Gardens, you can view a life-size replica of a sei whale and the skeleton of a pilot whale and learn about marine creatures found in the waters off Nova Scotia. This large museum lets you explore the natural wonders of the province with exhibits on Sable Island, rocky ocean shores, and native mammals and birds. Visitors can sign up for the annual field trip known as the "Salamander Meander," meet the resident gopher tortoise, Gus, who is nearly one hundred years old, or see the rib of a blue whale. The museum has lots of things to catch the interest of whale-watchers of all ages.

Yarmouth County Museum (Yarmouth)

yarmouthcountymuseum.ca

This museum at the southern tip of Nova Scotia specializes in artifacts related to the seagoing heritage of this part of the province. Here you can see examples of scrimshaw and other treasures brought home from distant ports by local seafarers.

Sweeney Fisheries Museum (Yarmouth)

sweeneyfisheriesmuseum.ca

In this interactive museum, visitors can walk through a coastal freighter and see what it is like on a ship.

Prince Edward Island

Atlantic Veterinary College at the University of Prince Edward Island (Charlottetown)

upei.ca

Visitors may soon get to see the reassembled skeleton of a minke whale that washed ashore on PEI in 2010. Plans are underway to have the skeleton on display in the atrium of the vet school's learning commons by the fall of 2019. Check out page 35 to read more about the lead role AVC staff played in the necropsies of some of the NARWs who died in the summer of 2017.

Newfoundland and Labrador

Red Bay Whaling Station UNESCO World Heritage Site (Red Bay, Labrador)

redbay.info@pc.gc.ca & newfoundlandlabrador.com/top-destinations/red-bay

Red Bay, on the coast of Labrador, just across from the tip of Newfoundland, is known as the whaling capital of the world. In the 1500–1600s Basque whalers set up camp there to process whale blubber prior to shipping it back to Europe. Red Bay was named a National Historic Site in 1979 and a UNESCO World Heritage Site in 2013. When you get to Red Bay, you will see remnants of the red clay tiles that once belonged to the ovens where the Baques processed the blubber, and a chalup—the small open dory they used. Keep an eye out for the whale bones that still litter the beaches. In the Red Bay town hall, you will find the Right Whale Exhibit Museum and a four-hundred-year-old whale skeleton. A visit here would certainly tick off a bucket-list item for the dedicated whale fan.

Dr. Jon Lien Humpback Whale Pavilion (King's Point)

@whalekp on Twitter

King's Point in Green Bay, not far from the community of Springdale, claims to be the home of the world's largest reconstruction of a humpback whale. Right outside the Dr. Jon Lien Humpback Whale Pavilion, you may view icebergs and live whales in the water. Visitors to the town will want to take a photo of the whale tail sculpture and visit the King's Point Pottery Craft Gallery to check out the amazing work by local artisans, many with a whale theme. The recreated Viking settlement at L'Anse aux Meadows, another UNESCO World Heritage Site, is only a few hours away.

Memorial University of Newfoundland (St. John's)

mun.ca/csf

Plans are underway here to display the skeleton of a blue whale that washed ashore in Rocky Harbour in 2014. It will be the focal point of the new Core Science facility scheduled to open in 2020. Another blue whale that washed ashore that same year was preserved and displayed by the Royal Ontario Museum.

Petty Harbour Mini Aquarium (Petty Harbour)

miniaqua.org

Located just 15 minutes outside St. John's, people of all ages can get up close to all sorts of sea life found in the touch tank. The aquarium features different weekly themes where you can learn about things such as plastics in the ocean, invasive species, or plankton. The aquarium is open all summer.

TIMELINE

1000-1500 Basques begin whaling in waters off Europe

1500-1700 Basques begin whaling in waters off North America

1600s Other European nations begin commercial whaling

1600-1700 Whaling by Europeans living along the east coast of North America

1700-1860 New England whalers making 3–4-year whaling voyages to the Pacific Ocean

1851 Publication of *Moby Dick*

1880 First reports of ships hitting right whales

1902 International Council for the Exploration of the Seas (ICES), the first group to try to limit the exploitation of marine species, established

1924 League of Nations creates framework to regulate whaling

1931 Convention for the Regulation of Whaling signed by twenty-six nations

1935 Article 4, ban on all hunting of right whales and ban on killing of calves, juveniles, and females with calves of all species of whales

1935 Whalers begin to be paid a fixed salary, rather than based on catch, to prevent killing more whales than could be processed

1937 Ban on hunting right whales goes into effect and protection extended to gray whales

1946 International Convention for the Regulation of Whaling of 1946

1948 Article 3 establishes the International Whaling Commission (IWC)

1949 IWC meets to set limits on whaling

1950-72   Honour system created where each country is to monitor and enforce the ban. During this time hundreds of right whales are illegally killed in Bering Sea and off Argentina, South Africa, and in the Indian Ocean

1955   Right whales first reported in Cape Cod Bay

1960s   Environmental movement comes of age; concern over killing of whales is a key factor

1965-66   Right whales reported in Bay of Fundy by UNB Wildlife Biologists Bruce Wright and David Neave

1970s   Concerns begin about pollution and human effects on ocean

1970   US government creates NOAA (National Oceanographic and Atmospheric Administration)

1970s   US government enacts various legislation to protect endangered species, fish, and the environment

1971   Greenpeace founded in Vancouver, eventually acting against industrial whaling

1972   Appointment of International Whaling Observers by IWC

1972   Canada bans commercial whaling

1977   COSEWIC (Committee on the Status of Endangered Wildlife in Canada), an independent group of scientists and experts, is formed to advise the government of Canada on species at risk of extinction

1978   Jon Lien, Memorial University of Newfoundland, frees a whale from fishing nets

1978-82   CeTap (Cetacean and Turtle Assessment Program) aerial surveys conducted

1980s   Realization that North Pacific right whale and North Atlantic right whale are two of the most endangered animals in the world

1981   Grand Manan Whale and Seabird Research Station (GMWSRS) founded by David Gaskin

1982   Government of Canada enacts Canadian Whale Protection Regulations

1983	New England Aquarium (NEAq) hosts workshop on status of NARW
1986	IWC moratorium on all commercial whaling enacted
1986	NARW consortium of scientists formed to hold annual meetings, manage and share data
1990s	Debate over moratorium, division between pro- and anti-whaling countries
1990	Development of stronger ropes used in fishery; beginning of severe entanglements
1991	First US right whale Recovery Plan adopted by US government
1992	Delilah killed by ship strike off Grand Manan and necropsied by international team; efforts to move shipping lanes in the Bay of Fundy follow after more local right whale deaths in 1995 and 1997
1993	Canadian government designates the Bay of Fundy as a NARW conservation area
1994	US government designates three NARW critical habitat areas (calving grounds off Georgia/Florida, Cape Cod Bay, and Great South Channel)
1996	US government establishes rule to keep people 500 yards from NARW
1996	Establishment of Marine Stewardship Council to promote sustainable fisheries
1997	North Atlantic Right Whale Consortium (NARWC) shares access to data, with goal of eliminating human causes of NARW mortality
1997	Canadian Whale Institute (CWI) established
2000	Scientists recognize that there are three different species of right whales
2000	Only one NARW calf is born and adults appear thin and in poor health
2000	Beginning of rules to limit ship speed and move shipping lanes by IMO (International Maritime Organization, a part of UN that regulates shipping)
2000	Canada publishes first right whale recovery plan, prepared by the North Atlantic Right Whale Recovery Team, for World Wildlife Fund Canada and the Department of Fisheries and Oceans.

2002	Campobello Whale Rescue Team co-founded by Joe Howlett and Captain Mackie Greene
2004	Government of Canada begins enforcement of Species At Risk Act (SARA) to protect endangered species and their habitats
2003	Shipping lanes in Bay of Fundy moved away from right whale area, sanctioned by the International Maritime Organization and implemented by Canadian government
2005	Groups fight for reduced ship speeds in areas used by NARWs
2007-8	NOAA introduces strategy to reduce ship strikes by reducing ship speed, changing shipping lanes, and recommending ATBA (areas to be avoided) in US waters
2008	An ATBA sanctioned by the International Maritimes Organization to direct vessel traffic around the right whale critical habitat on Roseway Basin, south of Nova Scotia
2009	US government implements rules to limit groundlines in fishery
2009	DFO publishes SARA-compliant recovery strategy (Recovery Strategy for the North Atlantic Right Whale (*Eubalaena glacialis*) in Atlantic Canadian Waters [Final]. Species at Risk Act Recovery Strategy Series. Fisheries and Oceans Canada)
2014	DFO revises recovery strategy to include justification of two right whale critical habitat areas. (Fisheries and Oceans Canada. 2014. Recovery Strategy for the North Atlantic Right Whale (*Eubalaena glacialis*) in Atlantic Canadian Waters [Final]. Species at Risk Act Recovery Strategy Series)
2015	US government implements further rules to fishery, although most scientists consider them ineffective
2017	UME (Unusual Mortality Event): 17 NARWs are killed
2017	Whale rescuer Joe Howlett killed while freeing an entangled NARW
2017	Government of Canada suspends permission to disentangle all whales

2017-18	No NARW calves born
2018	Government of Canada implements "tackle box" approach with a variety of measures that can be implemented to help protect the NARW
2018	Government of Canada introduces measures to make whale disentanglement safer
2018	In December, a new NARW calf is born in the waters off Florida
2019	Six more calves seen by the middle of February—7 so far, not the baby boom that is needed

ACKNOWLEDGEMENTS

Thanks to the many experts who patiently answered my questions and made sure that I got the facts straight, especially: Dr. Moira Brown, Canadian Whale Institute; Dr. Donald McAlpine, New Brunswick Museum; Laurie Murison, Grand Manan Whale and Seabird Research Station; Dr. Kim Davies, Dalhousie University; Shelley Lonergan, Brier Island Whale and Seabird Cruises; Captain Mackie Greene, Island Cruises Whale Watch; Dr. Sean Brillant, Canadian Wildlife Federation; Jackie Walker and Cynthia Callahan, Hunstman Marine Science Centre.

Many other people helped me track down info and photos and answered more questions: Stephanie Anthony, Ken Boehner, Paul Boehner, Lena Chown, Lynn Dorgan, Donna Gaudette Gavin, Fraser Gavin, Belle Hatfield, Debra Hamilton, Joanne Head, Catherine Hoyt, Lesley Wells. Staff of Nimbus Publishing, especially editor extraordinaire, Whitney Moran; designer, Jenn Embree; and proofreader, Angela Mombourquette. Staff of the Saint John Free Public Library, Fundy Library Region and New Brunswick Public Library Service. I also want to thank all of the passionate whale-watchers out there who write books and articles, post pictures and stories on social media, and share their enthusiasm about the North Atlantic right whale. I couldn't have done this book without the assistance of everyone mentioned here, and many others who helped without even realizing it; if there are any errors in this book, they are not responsible. A final word of thanks to everyone in my family. Nick, Alex, and Hope put up with my endless talk about all things related to whales. My sister Pat gave me the use of her beautiful home at the beach so I could focus on research and writing for an entire week. My mother, Norma, was always encouraging and supportive. I can always count on my brother Barry to ask me tough questions that get me digging deeper. My PEI cousins provided much-needed background about fishing and whale necropsies. Thanks!

SELECTED BIBLIOGRAPHY

"Never doubt that a small group of thoughtful, committed citizens can change the world."

–Margaret Mead

Print

Bateman, Tom. "Lobster fishery navigates choppy sea amid whale ban." *Telegraph-Journal*, June 26, 2018.

Brown, M. W., Fenton, D., Smedbol, K., Merriman, C., Robichaud-Leblanc, K., and Conway, J. D. 2009. Recovery Strategy for the North Atlantic Right Whale (*Eubalaena glacialis*) in Atlantic Canadian Waters. *Species at Risk Act Recovery Strategy Series*. Fisheries and Oceans Canada.

Clapham, Phil. *Right Whales: Natural History & Conservation*. Stillwater, MN: Voyageur Press, 2004.

Hoare, Philip. *The Whale: In Search of the Giants of the Sea*. New York: HarperCollins, 2010.

Horowitz, Joshua. *War of the Whales: A True Story*. New York: Simon & Schuster, 2015.

Hoyt, Erich. *The Whale Watcher's Handbook*. Markham, Ontario: Penguin, 1984.

———. *The Whales of Canada: An Equinox Wildlife Handbook*. Camden East, ON: Camden House Publishing, 1984.

Kraus, Scott, and Kenneth Mallory. *Disappearing Giants*. Charlestown, MA: Bunker Hill Publishing, 2003.

———. *The Search for the Right Whale*. New York: Crown, 1993.

Kraus, Scott D., and Rosalind Rolland, eds. *The Urban Whale: North Atlantic Right Whale at the Crossroads*. Cambridge, MA: Harvard University Press, 2007.

Kraus, Scott D., et al. "Recent Scientific Publications Cast Doubt on North Atlantic Right Whale Future." *Frontiers in Marine Science*, 3:317.

Laist, David W. *North Atlantic Right Whales: From Hunted Leviathan to Conservation Icon*. Baltimore: Johns Hopkins University Press, 2017.

Lawley, David. *A Guide to Whale Watching in the Maritimes*. Halifax: Nimbus Publishing, 1997.

Lien, Jon, and Steven Katona. *A Guide to the Photographic Identification of Individual Whales Based on their Natural and Acquired Markings*. St. John's, NL: Breakwater 1990.

McLeod, Brenna A. "Red Tiles and Baleen." *Newfoundland Quarterly*. 100.4, 2008, 16–19, 34–35.

North Atlantic Right Whale Recovery Team. *Canadian North Atlantic Right Whale Recovery Plan*. World Wildlife Fund Canada and the Department of Fisheries and Oceans, 2000.

Parks, Susan E. et al. "Occurrence, Composition, and Potential functions of NARW (*EG*) Surface Active Groups." *Marine Mammal Science*, 2007.

———. "The Gunshot Sound Produced by Male North Atlantic Right Whales (*Eubalaena Glacialis*) and its Potential Function in Reproductive Advertisement." *Marine Mammal Science*, July 2005.

Perrin, William F., B. Würsig, and J. G. M. Thewissen, eds. *Encyclopedia of Marine Mammals*. New York: Academic Press, 2002.

Pyenson, Nick. *Spying on Whales: The Past, Present, and Future of Earth's Most Awesome Creatures*. New York: Viking, 2018.

"Right Whale Report Card: The Population Decline Continues." *Right Whale News*, 26.3, December 2018.

Russell, Dick. *Eye of the Whale: Epic Passage from Baja to Siberia*. New York: Simon & Schuster, 2001.

Online

Bains, Camille. "New regulations to protect marine mammals in effect for all coasts in Canada." *Globe and Mail* online, July 11, 2018.

Bragg, Mary Ann. "Right whale researchers attempt to disentangle 'Kleenex.'" *Cape Cod Times* online, April 13, 2008.

Campenella, Emanuela. "Plastic pollution crisis: How waste end up in our oceans." *Global News*, June 17, 2018.

Canadian Press. "Crews try to free entangled North Atlantic right whale." *CBC News* online, April 18, 2018.

CBC News. "DFO orders 'hard pill to swallow' for N.B. Lobster fishermen, union says," June 16, 2018.

Fields, Helen. "Shh…Ocean Noises Stress Out Whales." *Science* online. February 7, 2012

Gillis, Maggie. "What's in your harbour? Scientist appalled by Newfoundland's underwater trash problem," *CBC News*, Nov. 22, 2017.

Jones, Lindsay. "Tech to the rescue: the race to save the right whales," *Globe and Mail* online, April 3, 2018.

Ross, Shane. "How fishermen are protecting whales—and helping landscapers," *CBC News*, July 22, 2018.

Withers, Paul. "Snow crab fishery's 'sustainable' label suspended in wake of whale deaths," *CBC News*, March 20, 2018.

INDEX

Unless otherwise specified, terms refer to North Atlantic right whale.
Page numbers in *italics* refer to images.
Index of Whale Names on next page.

INDEX OF WHALE NAMES